BEETHOVEN

THE CONCERTGOER'S COMPANIONS
SERIES EDITOR ALEC HYATT KING

BEETHOVEN

A biography, with a survey of
books, editions and recordings

by

ROSEMARY HUGHES

CLIVE BINGLEY LONDON

FIRST PUBLISHED 1970 BY CLIVE BINGLEY LTD
16 PEMBRIDGE ROAD LONDON W11
SET IN 10 ON 13 POINT LINOTYPE TIMES
AND PRINTED IN THE UK BY
THE CENTRAL PRESS (ABERDEEN) LTD
COPYRIGHT © ROSEMARY HUGHES 1970
ALL RIGHTS RESERVED
85157 070 4

CONTENTS

My grateful thanks are due to Dr Alan Tyson and Dr Margit Finda (Vienna) for help and information generously given, and to Miss A P Barnes, County Librarian, Miss M H Sanders of the County Library Headquarters, Worcester, and Mrs V M Couchman, Branch Librarian, Pershore, who went to great trouble to provide me with the material I needed.

The quotations in the first chapter from letters written by Beethoven are taken from *The letters of Beethoven,* which is described on page 51, by permission of the publishers.

ROSEMARY HUGHES

Beethoven's life

BONN—THE EARLY YEARS: The division of Germany and Italy in the eighteenth century into scores of independent states, large and small, although politically deadening, provided admirable conditions for the flowering of the arts. The building of a summer palace or the maintenance of an orchestra may have been more a matter of prestige than of true connoisseurship; but many of the princes of this epoch, from the Empress Maria Theresa and Frederick the Great of Prussia downwards, were not only music-lovers but accomplished performers. And for thousands of professional musicians—singers, instrumentalists, composers and men of the theatre—service in a princely musical establishment provided a tolerably satisfying and secure means of livelihood.

Among the principalities, lay and ecclesiastical, of what are now Germany and Austria, nominally bound together since the early Middle Ages in a loose confederation under their elected emperor, seven carried the title, and the nominal function, of Elector. One of these was the archbishopric of Cologne, although the archbishop himself had since the thirteenth century set up his court and seat of government in Bonn. In this little city, with its beautiful situation on the Rhine, the electoral court provided for its population (some nine thousand by the end of the eighteenth century) employment and a certain amount of artistic and intellectual activity.

The archbishops of Cologne were also bishops of Liège, and it may have been as a result of an episcopal visitation that a young bass singer in Liège cathedral choir was invited to join the musical establishment at Bonn, and was appointed a court musician there in 1733. This young Flemish musician, born in Malines, was to be the grandfather of the great composer who was named after him, Ludwig van Beethoven. He was a forceful personality, 'short of stature, muscular, with extremely animated eyes, and greatly respected as an artist'—so he was described by one who remembered him. In 1761 he became musical director to the court and was able to secure a position in the choir and orchestra for his son Johann, a talented violinist and tenor singer. His one sorrow was that his wife had become an alcoholic, and eventually had to be cared for in a convent.

It was the more unfortunate that when Johann eventually married, his father disapproved of the bride, as being of a lower social station, and would neither welcome the young couple to his house nor make his home with them. Johann and Maria Magdalena van Beethoven accordingly set up on their own in a tiny apartment at the back of a house in the Bonngasse. He was twenty seven, she, at twenty one, already a widow; her first husband had been a valet, her father had been in charge of the kitchens at one of the other electoral residences. They lost their first baby within a week of his birth. Their second son, Ludwig, was born on December 16 1770.

Before long they moved to a house in the Rheingasse, belonging to a family named Fischer who, long afterwards, remembered them in the first years of their 'righteous and peaceful' married life, punctual in paying their rent and baker's bills, and described the tall, slender young wife, with her aquiline nose and serious eyes, busying herself with sewing and knitting, and able to hold her own modestly but shrewdly in conversation. Her husband was regular in the performance of his duties as tenor singer at court and also had a considerable teaching practice. Fischer added that ' he often had more to do than he could manage '. Perhaps there is a hint here of the trouble that overtook them, for all their promising start, and the slow drift into poverty and near squalor. For Johann drank: perhaps not greatly to excess at the outset, but increasingly as success eluded him and repeated applications for promotion or increase of salary were ignored. And Maria Magdalena lacked the vitality which might have enabled her to master the situation; probably she already carried the seeds of the tuberculosis of which she died. Quiet and unsmiling (the Fischers never remembered seeing her laugh) she struggled on, but she began to lose her grip, and Ludwig, now the eldest of three brothers, was remembered at school as being dirty and neglected in appearance.

Formal schooling played a relatively small part in his education, however, for his father had discovered his musical capacities and had been giving him lessons on the clavier since he was about five. The exact date cannot be determined; Johann, bent on exploiting him as a prodigy, persistently knocked two years off his age, so that Ludwig himself, until he was forty, believed that he had been born in 1772. In 1778 his father produced him at a concert, together with one of the court singers whom he had trained, as 'his little son of six years'. Nothing further is known about this, his first public appearance.

Further musical training was intensive but erratic. A cousin of his mother's, young Franz Rovantini, who lodged in the house and played in the court orchestra, taught him the violin and viola, and from 1779 Tobias Pfeiffer, also an inmate of the house, a fine pianist and wind player and a thoroughly unstable character, gave him piano lessons, sometimes late at night when he and Johann came home together after an evening's drinking. There was also a little instruction on the organ.

But the real turning point in his musical formation was when Christian Gottlob Neefe took him on as a pupil. Neefe had come to Bonn as musical director to a theatrical company, and had been appointed court organist in 1781. He was a gifted composer and a man of character and personality, for he held his post as organist, and was confirmed in it, in spite of representations against him on the grounds that he was a calvinist. Neefe set his pupil to work on Bach's *Well-tempered clavier* and gave him his first regular teaching in composition. So quick was the boy's response to sound tuition that before he was twelve he was able to take charge of the chapel services in Neefe's absence, and when, in 1783, Neefe took over the theatre, he put Ludwig in as 'cembalist to the orchestra', which involved all the rehearsal

9

work for stage performances. This was the year in which Neefe, contributing an account of the musical life and notabilities of Bonn to Cramer's *Magazin der Musik*, described Ludwig as: 'a boy of eleven years and of most promising talent. He plays the clavier very skilfully and with power, reads at sight very well, and—to put it in a nutshell—he plays chiefly the *Well-tempered clavier* of Sebastian Bach, which Herr Neefe put into his hands . . . So far as his duties permitted, Herr Neefe has also given him instruction in thorough-bass . . . This youthful genius is deserving of help to enable him to travel. He would surely become a second Wolfgang Amadeus Mozart were he to continue as he has begun.'

In 1784, at the age of thirteen, he was formally appointed assistant court organist; 'in case of need he has filled the place for nearly a year very well', according to an official report.

This official report was drawn up on the orders of the new elector, Maximilian Franz, who in April 1784 had succeeded to the archbishopric. He was an Archduke of Austria, son of Maria Theresa and brother of Marie Antoinette, Queen of France. In his short reign of ten years, before his electorate, like so many other German principalities, was submerged by the wars arising out of the French revolution, he made Bonn a centre of culture and education and new ideas as well as music. He brought with him a breath of the progressive spirit that was abroad at that time among liberal minded catholics, clergy and laity alike, and ordered the seminary in Cologne to adopt an improved course of theological training, beside founding new schools and raising the Bonn *Hochschule* to the rank of a university.

Ludwig was now, at thirteen, a salaried musician. But the poverty of his family, the growing incapacity of his father to provide and his mother to manage, made it desirable for him to augment his small salary. Teaching was the obvious answer. He hated it, yet it was to bring him one of the happiest and most formative relationships of his life when his friend Franz Wegeler, a young medical student, introduced him to the von Breuning family. Frau von Breuning, the widow of a court councillor, had been left with a growing family to bring up, and shared her pleasant house in the Münsterplatz with her two brothers, canons of the cathedral and men of culture, who gave the four children their education. Ludwig gave lessons to Eleonore, the eldest of the family, who was a year younger than himself, and to the youngest boy Lorenz. In the process, according to Wegeler, whom Eleonore was later to marry, he 'received his first acquaintance with German literature, especially poetry, as well as his first training in social behaviour'. Frau von Breuning in fact drew him into the family and gave him a little gentle discipline and a home where, as Wegeler said, 'everything conspired to make him cheerful and develop his mind'. His friendships with Wegeler and the young Breunings stood the strains put upon them by his difficult temperament and sometimes outrageous behaviour, and lasted to the end of his life.

In the spring of 1787, when Beethoven was sixteen, came his first glimpse of the larger musical world, a journey to Vienna. Whether he was subsidised by the Elector or by any of his friends is not known. He had a single, unforgettable glimpse of Joseph II, the liberalising emperor whom he venerated, and was introduced to Mozart, with whom he hoped to study. It is related that Mozart was unimpressed by his first improvisation, thinking it was a prepared show piece. But when the boy, stung by this, demanded a theme, he went on to improvise on it with such fire that Mozart listened with growing absorption and said to friends of his in an adjoining room 'Keep your eyes on him; some day he will give the world something to talk about'. The lessons with Mozart were begun; but less than a fortnight later Beethoven was hurrying home. His mother was very ill with consumption and his father had sent for him. He reached home to find her still living, and for a couple of months she lingered on, but in July she died. 'She was such a dear, kind mother to me, my best friend', he wrote to a friend in Augsburg from whom he had been obliged to borrow money in order to finish his journey. He was indeed in grave trouble. His father had sold or pawned many of their belongings during his mother's illness, he himself had used up his own small resources on the Vienna trip, and in addition was ill with asthma and haunted by the fear that he was perhaps consumptive like his mother.

11

Friends came to his rescue with affection, practical help, money. When, years later, the court violinist Franz Ries sent his son Ferdinand to him in Vienna with a letter of introduction, Beethoven replied 'I cannot answer your father's letter just now, but you write and tell him that I have not forgotten how my mother died. He will be satisfied with that'. Somehow the household struggled on, with a housekeeper to look after the three boys and their increasingly incapacitated father. At length, in 1789, Johann was retired, half of his pay being allocated to Ludwig, for the maintenance of the younger boys; this, at least, was the arrangement, but in a later petition Ludwig stated that his father had begged him not to enforce it, lest he should be publicly regarded as incapable of supporting his family, and had, himself, regularly made over half his pay to him in quarterly instalments. There is a real pathos in the father's sense of shame, as there is in the protective loyalty of Ludwig and his brothers, coaxing their father home from taverns and fighting to rescue him from the police.

In such a situation the refuge and companionship provided by the Breunings was beyond price. It may have been there that he struck up a new friendship. Count Ferdinand von Waldstein had come to Bonn in 1787 to enter the Teutonic Order, a venerable order of religious chivalry surviving from the Middle Ages, of which the Elector Max Franz was grand master. Eight years older than Beethoven and passionately musical, he was quick to sense Beethoven's quality. He visited him, made music with him, urged him on to improvise variations, gave him a piano; money had to be given under the guise of a gratuity from the Elector, to spare his pride. Beethoven's natural buoyancy reasserted itself. He attended a few university lectures, met his friends in such haunts of the young intelligentsia as Frau Koch's *Zehrgarten*, duly worshipped her beautiful and gifted daughter Babette, and experienced his first brief love affairs.

In 1788 Max Franz went ahead with his projected court theatre, engaging actors and singers and an orchestra of thirty one first class players, almost all young men; Beethoven was one of the viola players, and in 1789 was formally appointed as chamber musician. In the company of this excellent team, which was considered by some to rank with the famous Mannheim orchestra, he played his way, in the next few years, through a wide cross-section of the operatic repertory of the day. Further opportunities were provided by the Teutonic Order. There was the chivalric ballet which Count Waldstein devised for the carnival of 1791, danced by the local nobility in medieval costume; the music was supposed to be the Count's, but in fact Beethoven had written it for him. Then, in the autumn of the same year, Max Franz journeyed up the Rhine to preside over a gathering of the order at Mergentheim, and took his orchestra with him. This river trip in holiday mood also brought Beethoven the opportunity of hearing the famous Abbé Sterkel play. It was the first time he had heard a true keyboard virtuoso, and he was fascinated. When, in reply to the older man's friendly challenge, he sat down to play his own fiendishly difficult variations on Righini's 'Venni amore' he astonished his hearers by moulding his own powerful but un-polished style to the refined brilliance of Sterkel's.

But the most important contact of these years was made when Haydn passed through Bonn on his way to and from London, late in 1790 and in the summer of 1792, and on the latter journey agreed to take Beethoven as his pupil. By the autumn Beethoven had been granted leave of absence with pay and a subsidy (possibly at the instance of Count Waldstein), and was able to plan his journey and make his farewells. Times were troubled. War had been declared by Austria on revolutionary France, and by October the French were in occupation of a large part of the left bank of the Rhine; in his travel notebook Beethoven records that he tipped the postillion ' because the fellow drove us at the risk of a cudgelling right through the Hessian army going like the devil '. He left Bonn, never to return, in the first days of November, and by November 10 he was in Vienna.

IN VIENNA : THE RISING VIRTUOSO
To the young Rhinelander the imperial capital offered professional opportunity and social contacts on a scale beyond anything he had known before, even though, in the realm of ideas, the liberal electorate compared favourably with censorship-ridden

13

Austria. True, in the sphere of church music and opera the difference was mainly one of quantity; a comparison between the Viennese court opera and that maintained by successive archbishops in Bonn shows the latter to have ranged wider in its choices, including French *opéra comique* and German *Singspiel* alongside the prime favourites among the Italians. In Vienna, on the other hand, the scales were weighted heavily in favour of the Italians by the predilection of successive emperors, and it was only Schikaneder's Theater auf der Wieden, to which *The magic flute* had brought prosperity, that still offered a home to opera in German. Public concerts were comparatively rare events. There were the four annual performances in the court theatre in aid of musicians' widows and orphans, at which the most distinguished performers of the capital gave their services; in his latter years Haydn repeatedly conducted his great choral works at these concerts and thereby raised large sums for the fund. There were also occasional benefit concerts, but hardly any subscription series such as London knew. But London's concert life was the joint product of its titled people and its wealthy mercantile middle class, whereas in Vienna the great aristocrats maintained their own musical establishments, from a string quartet to a full orchestra.

Here, for the young professional musician, was the field of opportunity. The nobility played and sang themselves, arranged concerts among their circle, subscribed for the latest sonatas and chamber music, and would often commission music for their own exclusive use. Their lead was followed by merchants and professional people of wealth and culture. These were the circles which the young Beethoven, thanks to the contacts which the Elector and Count Waldstein provided for him, was at once able to enter.

His first weeks were spent in finding lodgings, purchasing the necessary equipment for his new professional and social life, from a piano to black silk stockings, and contacting Haydn, with whom he was to study. The lessons were duly begun, but it was not long before he discovered that Haydn, like many great creative artists, was no teacher. Strict academic counterpoint based on Fux's famous *Gradus ad Parnassum* was the basic technical discipline for a young composer, but Beethoven found that Haydn was not taking him through it fast enough nor consistently correcting his mistakes. Through the Abbé Gelinek, one of the established musicians of the city, he was introduced to another teacher, Johann Schenk, and began taking lessons with him as well. As Schenk, out of professional delicacy, insisted that this should be kept secret, Beethoven obediently copied Schenk's corrections into the exercises he laid before the unsuspecting Haydn. Haydn was duly delighted with his work, and glowing accounts of his progress filtered through to Bonn.

But relations between Haydn and his pupil were never easy, though Haydn obviously admired him and proved it by suggesting that Beethoven should accompany him on his second visit to England. He further showed his goodwill by writing an outspoken letter to the Elector, saying that Beethoven was not receiving enough money to live on in Vienna and that he had himself advanced him five hundred florins; with the letter he enclosed a selection of manuscripts as proof of his pupil's diligence. A tart reply from the Elector, pointing out that with two exceptions all the works in question had been composed before Beethoven left Bonn, made both Haydn and Beethoven look foolish, whether the misunderstanding was caused by any lack of frankness on Beethoven's part or merely by Haydn's failing to make sure of his facts before writing. Possibly as a result of this, Haydn went off to England without Beethoven, and Beethoven betook himself to the great theorist Albrechtsberger for counterpoint lessons. The suggestion may have come from Haydn, for Albrechtsberger was an old friend of his; if so, it was the best thing he ever did for Beethoven, for Albrechtsberger put him through the strict discipline he knew he needed even though he kicked against it. He also took lessons in the setting of Italian texts with Mozart's old rival Salieri, who generously gave free tuition to struggling composers as his time allowed.

Meanwhile his reputation as a performer was spreading, enhanced by those salon contests between virtuosi (then much in vogue) such as that in which he completely outplayed and outimprovised the brilliant Abbé Gelinek; it speaks well for Gelinek's good nature that he still took so much to heart Beethoven's frustration with Haydn's teaching as to introduce him to Schenk. His playing of Bach, on whose keyboard music his earliest training and reputation had been grounded, also won him friends. The Baron van Swieten, great lover of Bach and Handel and somewhat pedantic patron of Mozart and Haydn, would issue an invitation with instructions to come prepared to stay the night, and Prince Karl Lichnowsky, who held chamber music parties at his house every Friday morning, was so impressed with Beethoven that before long he had invited him to become a member of his household.

This arrangement did not last long. Beethoven could not bear the discipline of regular hours and compulsory sociability and very soon found himself an independent lodging once more. That he retained the friendship and admiration of Prince Lichnowsky and a widening circle of the Austrian nobility, in spite of behaviour on his part that ranged from the offhand to downright insult, does honour to their musical judgment, their humanity and their capacity to distinguish the behaviour from the person. The Austrian upper classes were in fact a profoundly civilised society, in which energy and idealism were channelled into the arts and not, as in contemporary England, into public and political life.

Further success was not long in coming to Beethoven. In 1795 he made his first public concert appearances, at the annual charity concerts and at Haydn's benefit. He also published his opus 1, three piano trios, for which there were 250 subscribers. Haydn, who had advised him not to publish the third trio, in C minor, later admitted to Beethoven's pupil Ries that he had not thought they would be so well received; his advice was certainly due to anxiety on this score, and not, as Beethoven suspected, to jealousy.

In the following year Beethoven undertook two concert tours, to Prague, Dresden and Berlin, and later to Hungary. To his hearers in these cities, as in Vienna, he brought a new experience of what piano playing could be, even to those among them who had heard Mozart. This must be seen in relation to the development of the still youthful pianoforte in the last quarter of the eighteenth century, when, Czerny tells us, the capacities of the instrument and the current fashion led to a 'choppy, short, detached ' style of playing. Mozart himself, as his letters show, looked not only for power and brilliance in an instrument but also for sustaining power. In this context one of Beethoven's letters is revealing, the more so as it is written to the piano maker Andreas Streicher, son-in-law and successor to Johann Andreas Stein whose instruments Mozart so greatly admired. The letter probably dates from the year of his concert tour: ' There is no doubt that so far as the manner of playing is concerned, the *pianoforte* is still the least studied and developed of all instruments; often one thinks that one is merely listening to a harp. And I am delighted, my dear fellow, that you are one of the few who realise and perceive that, provided one can feel the music, one can also make the pianoforte sing. I hope that the time will come when the harp and the pianoforte will be treated as two entirely different instruments.'

Clearly it was his legato playing, and the resultant singing tone, which Czerny tells us he commanded ' to an incomparable degree ', that enchanted listeners by its sheer beauty and at the same time carried the instrument and its literature towards a fresh stage of development.

But it was his power of improvisation, of extemporaneous creation at the keyboard, which moved his first audiences most deeply. This was an art of honourable lineage, belonging to the days before the mass production of printed music and now lost save in the hands of a few organists of the highest rank. An anonymous contributor to a Leipzig periodical, the *Allgemeine musikalische Zeitung,* wrote that ' since the death of Mozart, who in this respect is for me still the *non plus ultra,* I have never enjoyed this kind of pleasure in the degree in which it is provided by Beethoven ', and J B Cramer, Beethoven's younger rival and friend, who made his honourable career in London, would say in later years that ' no man in these days has heard extempore playing, unless he has heard Beethoven '.

All this was happening against a background of a continent in turmoil and a country at war. Already in 1794 the Rhineland had been finally overrun by the French armies and the Elector Max Franz driven from Bonn; his principality was incorporated in the

17

French republic three years later and he himself, a princely refugee, eventually settled in Vienna. The war had also brought to Vienna a number of Beethoven's old friends from Bonn—Count Waldstein and Franz Wegeler, Stephan and Lorenz von Breuning, and Beethoven's own younger brother Johann, who took a job in an apothecary's shop. The elder brother, Caspar Carl, had already arrived in 1794 and was making a modest living as a teacher of music. So far Vienna itself had felt merely the backwash of either the war or the ideas behind the French revolution. But the emergence of the young Bonaparte as the inspired leader of the republic's armies brought a new threat to Austria as he thrust northwards from Italy. The rising danger was mirrored in a stream of patriotic songs, to which Beethoven contributed but of which one alone has endured, Haydn's 'Emperor's hymn'. Austria was driven to make peace at Campo Formio in 1797, and the spring of 1798 saw the arrival as French ambassador in Vienna of one of Napoleon's generals, Jean Baptiste Bernadotte. A man of culture and ability (his suite included the violinist Rodolphe Kreutzer), he became a centre of attraction, during his brief sojourn, for those to whom France was not merely a victorious enemy, murderous and subversive, but also a spring of vitalising ideas, with Bonaparte as liberator. Beethoven was among these, and many years later his friend and factotum Schindler stated that it was Bernadotte who first suggested Bonaparte to Beethoven as the subject of a 'heroic' symphony.

At this point Beethoven seemed to have the world at his feet. He and his two brothers were established in Vienna in honourable independence: his own fame was growing. In 1800, the last year of the century and his own thirtieth, he produced his first symphony at the first concert he gave entirely on his own account; it was in April, at the Court theatre. A set of string quartets was ready for publication, and he had enriched his own instrument with three concertos, a number of chamber works with piano, and a baker's dozen of solo sonatas; the most recent of these, opus 22, he was particularly pleased with, and told his publisher that it had 'turned out a treat'. Prince Lichnowsky was paying him an annual sum of 600 gulden, and he could command his price for new compositions. Princely patrons like Lichnowsky and the openhanded young Lobkowitz were among his friends, as were many amateur musicians such as Karl Amenda, tutor to the Lobkowitz children, and Baron Zmeskall von Domanowecz, civil servant and cellist, who cut his quill pens for him and endured his merciless teasing; so, too, were professional colleagues like Ignaz Schuppanzigh, leader of Prince Lichnowsky's quartet team, a stout young man whom he nicknamed 'Falstaff' and who became the first interpreter of his string quartets. His only worry was his health. He was naturally robust, but he had a chronic abdominal weakness that manifested itself in wearing bouts of diarrhoea. And another cloud, as yet no bigger than a man's hand, was soon to spread and darken his entire firmament.

ONSET OF DEAFNESS
The cause of Beethoven's deafness is still debated by specialists. Even the date of its onset is uncertain. Beethoven himself had begun to notice the first signs of it by 1799, but said nothing about them. He himself seems to have believed that it was in some way connected with his chronic diarrhoea, and had himself treated for that, only to find that even when the diarrhoea was relieved the deafness persisted. By 1801 he was seriously worried, as can be seen from his letters to Amenda and to his old friend Wegeler, now once more in Bonn. Beethoven went from doctor to doctor, asked Wegeler his professional opinion of various specialists and treatments, including galvanism, and avoided social gatherings for fear of his deafness becoming public property. For anyone to shout at him not only betrayed his secret but also caused him acute physical discomfort. He thought of travel and asked Amenda to come with him on a concert tour, explaining that 'my trouble makes itself felt least in my playing and composing, most in social intercourse'.

Since 1800 he had been in the habit of spending the summer months in rented rooms outside Vienna, where he could work undisturbed and refresh his spirit by long walks in the wooded hills and valleys he loved. In the summer of 1802 he found lodgings in the village of Heiligenstadt, and settled down to work on his second symphony. Among his summer visitors was young Ferdinand Ries from Bonn, whom he had taken on as a pupil out of gratitude for his father's help and kindness in the past. On one of their walks together Ries called Beethoven's attention to a shepherd who had been playing his pipe among the trees for the past half hour. Beethoven had heard nothing, and though Ries tried to patch up his blunder by assuring his master that he too could not hear it, Beethoven fell into a stricken silence. In the loneliness of the ensuing autumn, forced to recognise that his deafness was progressive and probably incurable, he stood face to face with his trouble. Death, through illness or even by his own hand, suddenly loomed in the foreground of his mind. He sat down to make his will, and poured out on to paper that letter, found in his desk after his death nearly a quarter of a century later, which we know as the Heiligenstadt testament. In its incoherence, even in its stilted phraseology, it bears witness to the depth of the darkness that had engulfed him in those few October days and to the passionate urge to communicate which is an essential feature of his make-up as man and artist.

Heiligenstadt, 6 October 1802
For my Brothers Carl and (Johann) Beethoven
O my fellow men, who consider me, or describe me as, unfriendly, peevish or even misanthropic, how greatly do you wrong me. For you do not know the secret reason why I appear to you to be so . . . just think, for the last six years I have been afflicted with an incurable complaint which has been made worse by incompetent doctors. From year to year my hopes of being cured have gradually been shattered and finally I have been forced to accept the prospect of a *permanent infirmity* . . . Though endowed with a passionate and lively temperament and even fond of the distractions offered by society I was soon obliged to seclude myself and live in solitude. If at times I decided just to ignore my infirmity, alas! how cruelly was I then driven back by the intensified sad experience of my poor hearing. Yet I could not bring myself to say to the people: 'Speak up, shout, for I am

20

deaf '. Alas! how could I possibly refer to the impairing *of a sense* which in me should be more perfectly developed than in other people, a sense which at one time I possessed in the greatest perfection . . . If I appear in company I am overcome by a burning anxiety, a fear that I am running the risk of letting people notice my condition—And that has been my experience during the last six months which I have spent in the country . . . how humiliated I have felt if somebody standing beside me heard the sound of a flute in the distance and *I heard nothing,* or if somebody heard a shepherd sing and again I heard nothing—Such experiences almost made me despair, and I was on the point of putting an end to my life—The only thing that held me back was *my art.* For indeed it seemed to me impossible to leave this world before I had produced all the works that I felt the urge to compose; and thus I have dragged on this miserable existence . . . I hope that I shall persist in my resolve to the end, until it pleases the inexorable Parcae to cut the thread; perhaps my condition will improve, perhaps not; at any rate I am now resigned—At the early age of 28 I was obliged to become a philosopher, though this was not easy; for indeed this is more difficult for an artist than for anyone else—Almighty God, who look down into my inmost soul, you see into my heart and you know that it is filled with love for humanity and a desire to do good. Oh my fellow men, when some day you read this statement, remember that you have done me wrong . . . And you, my brothers Carl and (Johann), when I am dead, request on my behalf Professor Schmidt, if he is still living, to describe my disease, and attach this written document to his record, so that after my death at any rate the world and I may be reconciled as far as possible—At the same time I herewith nominate you both heirs to my small property (if I may so describe it)—Divide it honestly, live in harmony and help one another . . . Well, that is all—joyfully I go to meet Death —should it come before I have had an opportunity of developing all my artistic gifts, then in spite of my hard fate it would still come too soon . . . Farewell; and when I am dead, do not wholly forget me. I deserve to be remembered by you, since during my lifetime I have often thought of you and tried to make you happy—Be happy—

LUDWIG VAN BEETHOVEN

Heiligenstadt, 10 October 1802—Thus I take leave of you —and, what is more, rather sadly—yes, the hope I cherished —the hope I brought with me here of being cured to a certain extent at any rate—that hope I must now abandon completely. As the autumn leaves fall and wither, likewise—that hope has faded for me. I am leaving here—almost in the same condition as I arrived—Even that high courage—which has often inspired me on fine summer days—has vanished—Oh Providence—do but grant me one day *of pure joy*—For so long now the inner echo of real joy has been unknown to me— Oh when—oh, when, Almighty God—shall I be able to hear and feel this echo again in the temple of Nature and in contact with humanity—Never?—No!—Oh, that would be too hard.

Later in October he returned to Vienna. Outwardly nothing seemed to have happened. He flung himself once again into his life of composing and teaching, carrying on zestful running fights with his publishers and planning and giving concerts. Early in 1803 Emanuel Schikaneder engaged him as resident composer at the handsome new Theater an der Wien, and in April he arranged a concert there for his own benefit, at which he played his C minor piano concerto and conducted the first and second symphonies and the first performance of his hurriedly written oratorio *Christus am Oelberge* (Christ on the Mount of Olives). In the following month he took part in the first performance of the 'Kreutzer' sonata with the mulatto violinist George Bridgetower. The work was only completed on the day of the performance, and Bridge-tower had to play the middle movement from Beethoven's own manuscript; it was originally dedicated to him, but according to Bridgetower the two men quarrelled over a girl and Beethoven then dedicated it to Rodolphe Kreutzer.

But beneath the surface there were profound changes. Already in 1801 he had told a friend that he was dissatisfied with what he

22

had done hitherto and that he intended from then on to take a new way. His pupil Czerny, who records this, sees the piano sonatas of op 31 as the first-fruits of this resolve, and he is probably right. But far greater than any measurable gap between these sonatas and their immediate predecessors is that between the first two symphonies and the towering work which, according to the sketchbooks, had begun to take shape in his mind before the end of 1802 and to which he was to devote months on end in 1803—months of relentless and self-disciplined labour that left him drained of energy and incapable of what is normally reckoned as self-discipline in other aspects of life.

It was also in 1803 that another break with his previous life occurred. He had been in love, the year before, with a ' dear, enchanting girl ', whom he speaks of in a letter as bringing him a few moments of happiness in the increasing isolation forced upon him by his deafness. This was probably his pupil, the youthful Countess Giulietta Guicciardi. She now became engaged to a man of her own age and station, Count Robert Gallenberg, himself a composer of ballet music, married him and left Vienna. There was no overt tragedy or rift between her and Beethoven, although he had believed that they loved each other. But a curious dialogue between Beethoven and Schindler, which took place through the medium of Beethoven's conversation pad over twenty years later, gives evidence of a final encounter, long believed, on Schindler's authority, to have occurred in 1821. If, however, Elliot Forbes[1] is right in setting aside Schindler's gloss, it happened before Giulietta left for Italy with Gallenberg, and is only less significant than Beethoven's own comment on it. He recalled that Giulietta had come to him in tears, and that he had repulsed her. When Schindler exclaimed ' Hercules at the crossroads!' Beethoven replied 'And if I had wished to give my vital powers with that life, what would have remained for the nobler, the better?' Even if this be wisdom after the event, it suggests a partial explanation of that fear of a fully self-giving relationship with a woman, which at the same time he so deeply longed for: a recognition, however

[1] *Thayer's life of Beethoven,* revised and edited by Elliot Forbes (1964), vol I pp 289-290.

obscure, that his was a vocation that demanded an undivided holocaust, no less than that of the mystic.

Not that in sexual matters Beethoven was a saint or ascetic, and his strongly passionate nature was frequently at war with his no less strong sense of the ugliness of promiscuity and the ideal beauty of faithful married love. But his purely physical affairs were relatively shortlived, and it was a point of principle with him never to compromise the honour of a married woman. This is perhaps the place to state that it appears highly unlikely that his deafness was caused by syphilis, or indeed that, as is sometimes rumoured, he had syphilis at all.

The new symphony was finished in the spring of 1804, and was still, in the mind of its creator, a ' Bonaparte ' symphony. But in May, as the work was being copied, Ries brought Beethoven the news that the First Consul had been proclaimed emperor, and describes how the composer tore up the title page of the copy destined for Paris, in a fury of disillusionment that the hero of the revolution had shown himself to be ' nothing more than an ordinary mortal ', ready to follow the path of ambition and tyranny. It was only after this that he gave it the title of ' heroic symphony '—*sinfonia eroica*. It was first rehearsed and performed privately, in the palace of Prince Lobkowitz. It was too new, the gap between it and the two earlier symphonies too vast, for it to be accepted immediately. But during the summer Prince Louis Ferdinand of Prussia (who, Beethoven used to say, would have been a very good musician if he had not been a prince) visited Prince Lobkowitz, listened with mounting excitement to a performance of the symphony and asked for it to be played again immediately, then, as he was leaving very shortly, for another repetition after that. Upon this, according to a contemporary, ' the impression made by the music was general and its lofty contents were now recognised '.

Meanwhile Beethoven had felt the recoil of this creative crisis, of which, also, the great C major sonata dedicated to his old friend and patron Count Waldstein was a by-product. In May he fell ill, and was nursed by the faithful Stephan von Breuning, now in the civil service, with whom he was sharing rooms. His convalescence was followed by a blazing quarrel with Breuning and his departure in a fury to spend the summer months, as usual, outside Vienna. 'For the life of me I should never have thought I could be so lazy as I am here', he wrote to Ries from the little spa at Baden. 'If an outbreak of really hard work is going to follow, then indeed something fine may be the result.' The 'laziness' was the trough between two waves; when Ries went out to him for a lesson later that summer he found him wrestling with the last movement of the sonata in F minor to which its publisher gave the title *Appassionata*.

He returned to Vienna in the autumn, met Breuning and made up their quarrel, and marked their reconciliation with the gift of a miniature of himself and a characteristic letter: 'Behind this painting, my dear good St[ephan], let us *conceal* forever *what passed between us* for a time.—I know that I have wounded *your heart;* but the emotion within me, which you must have certainly detected, has punished me sufficiently for doing so. . . . Forgive me if I hurt you. I myself suffered just as much. When I no longer saw you beside me for such a long time, only then did I realise to the full how dear you were to *my* heart, how dear you ever will be.'

Breuning, no less characteristically, wrote to Wegeler, who was now married to his sister Eleonore, describing his friend's condition but saying nothing about the quarrel: 'You cannot conceive, my dear Wegeler, what an indescribable, I might say fearful effect the gradual loss of his hearing has had upon him. Think of the feeling of being unhappy in one of such violent temperament; in addition reservedness, mistrust, often towards his best friends, in many things want of decision! For the greater part, with only an occasional exception when he gives free vent to his feelings on the spur of the moment, intercourse with him is a real exertion, at which one can scarcely trust to oneself. From May until the beginning of this month we lived in the same house, and at the outset I took him into my rooms. He had scarcely come before he became severely, almost dangerously ill, and this was followed by an intermittent fever. Worry and the care of him used me rather severely. Now he is completely well again . . . and as I am keeping house he eats with me every day.'

It was not the first nor the last time that Beethoven tried the patience and generosity of his friends almost to breaking point.

OPERATIC PROJECTS

If Beethoven's connection with opera is a tale of lengthy and largely unsuccessful courtship on his part, this must be seen in the setting of the predominant place held by the stage in the musical polity as the touchstone of artistic success and the source of prestige and money. It was a feather in his cap when, in 1800, and with no previous work for the stage to his credit, he was engaged to compose the music for a ballet for the Court theatre. This ballet, the work of the great choreographer Salvatore Viganò, was entitled *The creations of Prometheus* and, perhaps as a topical allusion to the persistent success of Haydn's *Creation*, took as its theme that portion of the Prometheus myth in which the Titan moulds men out of clay and then brings them to life and transports them to Parnassus to be enlightened by Apollo and the Muses. The ballet was first performed in March 1801 and by the end of the following year had received twenty three performances, which for those days was a marked success, and warranted the publication of a piano arrangement of the score.

The fusion, in Beethoven's mind, of the Prometheus image with that of Bonaparte as liberator, the identification of this idea with the theme of the closing number of the ballet, and its transmutation into the last movement of the *Eroica* symphony, were all part of the spiritual journey of the ensuing months.

Meanwhile, early in 1803, not long after he had moved into his quarters at Schikaneder's theatre, reports were afoot that he was about to compose an opera to a text by Schikaneder himself. In fact it was not until November 1804 that he started work in earnest on Schikaneder's text, *Vestas Feuer* ('The vestal flame'). Two months later he handed it back as being 'too thankless'; he had composed very little of it, but his sketchbooks show that he drew on it in composing *Fidelio*. Early in 1804 the growing competition presented by Schikaneder to the Court theatre came to a head when the manager of the theatre, Baron von Braun, bought up the Theater an der Wien and dismissed Schikaneder.

26

The change of management had ended Beethoven's contract with the theatre, but not before the seed had been sown which was to bear fruit in his only opera. Early in 1804 his letters show him at work on a libretto translated from the French, *Léonore ou l'amour conjugal*. It was based on a recent incident actually experienced by the librettist, J N Bouilly, a provincial administrator, during the revolutionary terror, in which a wife had rescued her husband from prison. Months later, when Schikaneder had been reinstated by his former rival von Braun as director of the theatre and was casting around for an attractive novelty, he turned to Beethoven, and before the year was out Beethoven was fully engaged on the opera, which during 1805 engulfed him as completely as the *Eroica* symphony had done in 1803-4. On every plane the subject held an irresistible attraction for him. The revolutionary and liberator in him responded to the theme of freedom regained, the figure of the heroic and faithful wife appealed to his strong vein of moral idealism, and in the prisoner Florestan (as has lately been suggested with great insight by Alan Tyson) he could see his own destiny and his response to it in ' the stoicism of isolation and silence '.[2] Throughout the summer he worked on it unremittingly, and in September it was put into rehearsal for performance on October 15, the name day of the Empress. Delays were caused by the censorship and by difficulties which arose over copying and rehearsing, and the first performance had to be postponed till November. But by then Napoleon's armies were in occupation of the capital, normal life was in abeyance and at the first three performances the house was either half empty or taken up by the occupying army.

Although, by a tragic irony, the armies of Napoleon's France had been in part responsible for the failure of *Fidelio*, it also contained structural defects springing from the modification of the original libretto by its translator. Those among Beethoven's friends who most valued his work and could see most clearly the grandeur of the finest scenes in the opera, were faced with the task of persuading him that some cuts and modifications were

[2] Alan Tyson, ' Beethoven's heroic phase ', *Musical times*, February 1969, 139-41.

necessary if there were to be any hope of reviving it. After a protracted and stormy session he was induced to yield. The consequent revision and telescoping of the first and second acts was undertaken by Stephan von Breuning and the opera was given again in the spring of 1806, this time with a new overture, the one known to us as 'Leonora no 3'. It was more successful, but Beethoven quarrelled with the management over the receipts and demanded his score back. It was not revived for eight years.

His immediate thanks to Stephan von Breuning for his tireless work on the revision of *Fidelio* took the form of a little song; but before the year was out he paid his friend the tribute he deserved with the dedication of the violin concerto, which was first performed (in fact, read at sight) by the violinist Clement at his benefit concert in December. The G major piano concerto and the fourth symphony were also composed during and immediately after his work on *Fidelio*; throughout his life the habit of working at several compositions at the same time brought about a constant cross-fertilisation between one work and another. It was in these years of intense creative energy that a commission from the Russian ambassador Count Rasoumofsky (who maintained a permanent string quartet led by Ignaz Schuppanzigh and himself played the violin) called forth the three great quartets which have immortalised his name.

FRIENDSHIPS AND LOVES

During these years, teaching, although he never liked it, provided money and such relaxation as comes from a change of occupation. Ferdinand Ries, indeed, he taught for nothing, out of gratitude to his father, and the young man made himself useful in countless ways, as did the boy Czerny. But the remunerative pupils, of course, came from the nobility and even from the imperial family. It was about this time that he began to give piano lessons to the Archduke Rudolph, a delicate and sensitive lad still in his teens. The relationship matured from that of master and pupil into a real friendship. The Archduke was a genuinely gifted pianist and composer and a sympathetic human being who was never put out by Beethoven's refusal to observe court etiquette in relation to him, and gave orders to his suite that they were not to insist on it.

Another instance in which the relationship between teacher and pupil led to a far deeper intimacy was that with the Brunsvik family. It was in 1799 that the two young countesses Therese and Josephine Brunsvik were brought to Vienna by their mother to be launched on society and receive the finishing touches to their education. For piano tuition no lesser person than Beethoven would do, and so, as Therese recalled, 'like a schoolgirl on her way to school, my copy of Beethoven's sonata with violin and cello accompaniment under my arm', she and her sister, escorted by their mother, climbed the three flights of stairs that led to Beethoven's apartment. The work she brought with her was probably one of the op 1 piano trios, of which she played the piano part and sang the violin and cello parts in turn. Delighted by this spirited performance, Beethoven agreed to teach the two sisters and came daily to their hotel suite, giving them hours of his time and 'never wearying of holding down and bending' her fingers, which she had previously been taught to hold flat. (This completely accords with Czerny's account of having been taught by him as a child 'something at the time still unknown to most players, the only correct position of the hands and fingers '.)

Beethoven soon became the friend and intimate of the entire Brunsvik family circle: the three girls, Therese, Josephine and Charlotte, their brother Franz, their aunts and their sprightly little cousin Giulietta Guicciardi. Musical gatherings in Vienna and summer visits to their country estate in Hungary cemented their friendship, which blazed up into the brief love affair between him and Giulietta. Meanwhile the second of the Brunsvik girls, the beautiful and sensitive Josephine, had been persuaded by her mother into reluctant marriage with a man much older than herself, Count Joseph Deym, the owner of a much visited collection of waxworks and casts. Early in 1804 he died, after less than five years of marriage, leaving Josephine in frail health, with four young children and a tangle of financial anxieties. During her brief married life Beethoven had continued to give her lessons. Now his visits became longer and more frequent, and we can watch the growth of a deepening love, certainly on his part and probably on hers, through the eyes of her sisters, anxious for their beloved Pepi's peace of mind: 'But tell me', writes Therese from home in January 1805, 'what is going to happen with Pepi and Beethoven? She must look out. I suppose it is with reference to her that you have underlined these words in the score you send me, "Her heart must have the strength to say No"'. And Beethoven's own letters to her, (discovered as recently as 1949) move swiftly from the pleasurable excitement of arranging musical evenings for her to outright confession: '. . . When I came to you—it was with the firm resolve not to let a single spark of love be kindled in me. But you have conquered me—The question is, whether *you wanted to do so*? or whether *you did not want to do so*? No doubt J(osephine) could answer that question for me some time—Dear God, there are so many more things I should love to tell you—how much I think of you—what I feel for you—but how weak and poor are those words—at any rate, my words—.'

Josephine on her part, torn between the demands of his intense devotion, the anxieties of her sisters and the needs of her young family, must have suffered all the distress of a gentle and conscientious nature to whom the pull of conflicting human claims and needs represents the keenest suffering that life can bring.

They remained in close contact during the summer of 1805, but in the autumn the advance of the French armies drove her to leave Vienna with her children for the family home in Hungary. When she returned to Vienna over a year later, they were both torn between a longing for the old loving intimacy and a growing recognition on her part that it could lead to nothing. At last her oversensitive heart found the strength to say no merely by refusing to see him: 'Since I must almost fear that you no longer *allow yourself to be found* by me—and since I do not care to put up with the refusals of your servant any longer—well then, I cannot come to you any more—unless you let me know what you think about this—Is it really *a fact*—that you do not want to see me any more —if so—do be *frank*? I certainly deserve that you should be frank with me . . . Do let me know, dear Josephine—what you think. Nothing shall bind you—In the circumstances I can and certainly dare not say anything more to you. All good wishes, dear, dear J(osephine).'

Of the later flowering of his relationship with Therese little is known with certainty. At the time of his love for Josephine his letters and references to her are all in a tone of affectionate family banter. But with her stormy, richly endowed nature and deep spirituality she was more closely akin to him in spirit than Josephine. A friend of the family believed that their relationship deepened into what was to be his profoundest love, and that they even became engaged, but that Beethoven could not make up his mind to get married. If this is true, it shows once more his psychological inability to surrender to a complete relationship with a woman, however much he longed for it, coupled with the indecision that often drove his friends to despair.

Between 1806 and 1809 he was at the height of his creative vitality and fame. He received commissions from aristocratic music lovers such as the Count Oppersdorf, to whom the fourth symphony is dedicated, and the younger Prince Nicholas Esterházy, the aged Haydn's master, who commissioned the Mass in C but did not care for it when he got it. His music was performed at private and charity concerts and was sought after by publishers as far afield as England. He was still able on occasion to appear in person to play or conduct, as he did at his own benefit concert in December 1808, at which his fifth and sixth symphonies were performed for the first time in public, and the Choral Fantasia, hurriedly composed for the occasion, received its première. But his deafness was a growing obstacle, and it is understandable that his petition for a permanent post at the imperial theatre was refused. In money matters he was a mixture of incompetence and fancied astuteness, suspiciousness and anxiety; he was not poor, at this point, by any standards, but he had no sense of security about his income. So when, in the autumn of 1808, he received the offer of the kapellmeistership at Cassel from Jerome Bonaparte, whom his brother Napoleon had made king of Westphalia, he considered the proposition seriously. His Viennese admirers and patrons were seriously alarmed at the idea of the greatest living composer—for he was already widely regarded as such—abandoning the imperial city, and for a provincial court under an upstart monarch. Accordingly three of them, Prince Lobkowitz, Prince Kinsky and the Archduke Rudolph himself, pooled their resources and offered him an annuity of three thousand florins if he would remain in Vienna. This he agreed to do, and refused the Cassel post.

The first months of 1809 were marked by a sequence of quarrels: with his friend Countess Erdödy, in whose house he had quarters, with the long suffering Stephan von Breuning, and with poor Ferdinand Ries, whom he suspected, quite baselessly, of intriguing to get the Cassel appointment while he himself was still considering it. (It would be worth attempting to trace whether his worst quarrels coincided with the periods of mental and physical exhaustion after a bout of intensive creative work.) May saw the French armies once more encircling Vienna, while Beethoven, sheltering in a cellar from the painful vibrations which the bombardment set up in his ears, worked at his fifth piano concerto. The imperial family, including the Archduke Rudolph, left the city; to mark the parting with his pupil and friend, Beethoven wrote the piano sonata op 81a, known as *Les adieux*, from the publisher's translation of the original German title. The other piano sonata of this year is that in F sharp major, op 78, dedicated to Therese Brunsvik. He is believed to have spent some weeks with the family that autumn, and if indeed his relationship with Therese deepened, it could well have been at this time.

In any event, the longing for marriage and a settled home was still strong within him. Early in 1810 he was drawn into contact with the musical and cultured Malfatti family by his friend Baron Ignaz von Gleichenstein, a fine amateur cellist for whom he had written the op 69 cello sonata and who was engaged to the younger of the two Malfatti daughters. Beethoven fell in love with the entire family. ' I am so happy when I am with them ', he wrote to Gleichenstein, ' I feel somehow that all the wounds which wicked people have inflicted on my soul could be cured by the Malfattis '. And the elder girl, Therese, aged nineteen, gay, lively and a gifted pianist, so captured his heart that he resolved to make an offer of marriage. In the end it appears that he asked Gleichenstein to take soundings, and that the result was unfavourable: ' If you would only be more candid; surely you are concealing something from me, and you want to spare me . . . Think and act for me—I dare not entrust to paper anything more of what I am thinking and feeling.' All that is known with certainty, however, is that Gleichenstein married Anna Malfatti, and remained Beethoven's friend, and that Therese, five years later, married the Baron von Drosdick.

A new friendship sprang up to distract his mind from this disappointment, with the visits of Bettina Brentano. She was the half sister of Franz Brentano, a business man from Frankfurt, who had married the daughter of the great Viennese scholar Joseph von Birkenstock and for some years made his home in his father in law's mansion. Beethoven was already acquainted with the family (and later dedicated his op 109 piano sonata to Franz's daughter), but his reputation for moodiness and inaccessibility was such that they hesitated to introduce him to Bettina when she came to visit them. She, however, was not to be denied, and boldly went to his rooms alone to introduce herself. She was a striking looking girl of twenty five, gifted and intuitive and already something of a writer and composer; her life was dominated by an adoring passion for Goethe, now sixty, who many years ago had loved her mother. This proved to be an immediate bond with Beethoven, who for years had read and honoured Goethe, and at the beginning of that year had been absorbed in the writing of the overture and incidental music to his *Egmont*. Her letters describing their successive meetings to Goethe and to others, highflown though their language is, make it clear that she had struck sparks from him, not least by her eager and unsentimental delight in the Goethe settings he sang to her. Catching her eye he said 'Aha—most people are touched by a good thing, but they are not artist natures. Artists are fiery, they do not weep.' To her he poured out his strong, formless, partly mystical conceptions of the nature of music and his own mission to mediate it to humanity. When, the next day, she showed him her record of their conversation, he exclaimed 'Did I say that? Well then, I had a raptus!'; but he did not disown it, and even made further notes for Goethe's benefit.

The personal meeting between Beethoven and Goethe which Bettina had so ardently wished to bring about took place two years later, at Teplitz, one of the spas to which his doctors sent him in 1811 and 1812; he had been persistently unwell for some time with his chronic bowel trouble and frequent disabling headaches. Bettina, who was now married to the poet Achim von Arnim, was in Teplitz with her husband, but was not present owing to a quarrel with Goethe's wife. The mutual understanding between the two great artists was not perfect, although Goethe was characteristically swift to grasp the essence of Beethoven's nature: 'Never before', he wrote 'have I seen an artist with more concentration, more energy, more inwardness'. But to Beethoven Goethe's response to his playing seemed strained and incomplete, and their divergent attitudes to courtly usage and to the great personages also in residence at Teplitz was a source of mutual irritation (even if, as seems probable, Bettina's frequently quoted story of their meeting with the Empress's suite and Beethoven's bad manners on that occasion contains more of fiction than fact). The two men remained in friendly contact, but as far as is known they never met again.

Teplitz brought Beethoven other agreeable friendships through the instrumentality of the young business man Franz Oliva who had accompanied him thither: the soldier poet Varnhagen von Ense, who was in Teplitz with the beautiful and brilliant Rahel Levin, whom he later married; the poet Tiedge, and the delightful young singer Amalie Sebald, with whom he appears to have had an amicable flirtation.

There is also evidence of a far deeper relationship in the famous letter to the unknown woman whom he calls his *unsterbliche Geliebte* ('immortal' or 'eternally' beloved). It was found in a secret drawer in his desk after his death; either he had never sent it, or it had been returned to him by the recipient.

July, 6, morning

My angel, my all, my very self.—Only a few words today, and, what is more, written in pencil (and with your pencil)—I shan't be certain of my rooms here until tomorrow; what an unnecessary waste of time is all this—Why this profound sorrow, when necessity speaks—can our love endure without sacrifices, without our demanding everything from one another;

34

can you alter the fact that you are not wholly mine, that I am not wholly yours? Dear God, look at Nature in all her beauty and set your heart at rest about what must be . . .

Monday evening, July 6th

You are suffering, you, my most precious one . . . Oh, where I am, you are with me—I will see to it that you and I, that I can live with you What a life! ! ! ! as it is now! ! ! ! without you—pursued by the kindness of people here and there, a kindness that I think—that I wish to deserve just at little as I deserve it—man's homage to man—that pains me—and when I consider myself in the setting of the universe, what am I and what is that man—whom one calls the greatest of men —and yet—on the other hand therein lies the divine element in man—I weep when I think that probably you will not receive the first news of me until Saturday—however much you love me—my love for you is even greater—but never conceal yourself from me—goodnight—as I am taking the baths I must get off to sleep—Dear God—so near! so far! Is not our love truly founded in heaven—and, what is more, as strongly cemented as the firmament of Heaven?—

Good morning, on July 7th

Even when I am in bed my thoughts rush to you, my eternally beloved, now and then joyfully, then again sadly, waiting to know whether Fate will hear our prayer—To face life I must live altogether with you or never see you . . . no other woman can ever possess my heart—never—never—Oh God, why must one be separated from her who is so dear. Yet my life in V(ienna) at present is a miserable life—Your love has made me both the happiest and the unhappiest of mortals—at my age I now need stability and regularity in my life—can this coexist with our relationship?—Angel, I have just heard that the post goes every day—and therefore I must close, so that you may receive the letter immediately—Be calm; for only by calmly considering our lives can we achieve our purpose to live together—Be calm—love me—Today—yesterday—what

35

tearful longing for you—for you—you—my life—my all—all good wishes to you—Oh, do continue to love me—never misjudge your lover's most faithful heart.

ever yours
ever mine   L.
ever ours

It has so far proved impossible to discover the identity of the woman to whom this letter was written (though the evidence of the complete document, of which excerpts only are given here, point to 1812 as the date). With Amalie Sebald, Beethoven's correspondence is in altogether lighter vein, and other incompatibilities appear to rule out the women whom he is known or believed to have loved most deeply—Giulietta Guicciardi, Josephine Deym, Therese Brunsvik. Perhaps it is fitting that, in this at least, we are not allowed to pluck out the heart of his mystery.

It was in any case a difficult time for him. His health was uncertain, and so was his income, for the Austrian government had been driven by its economic difficulties to devalue the currency, so that the annuity paid to him by the Archduke Rudolph and Princes Kinsky and Lobkowitz was reduced in value from 4,000 florins to just over 1,600. The Archduke immediately gave instructions that his share was to be brought up to the equivalent value in the new currency. But Kinsky was killed by a fall from his horse just as he had arranged to do likewise, and Lobkowitz was in financial trouble himself and unable to pay anything. Beethoven's incompetence in managing money, combined with his obsessive anxiety and suspiciousness, were the source of some of the most depressing and unworthy episodes in his life. It may have been unavoidable that he should take his claims on the Kinsky and Lobkowitz estates to the lawcourts, but the diatribes in his letters against the two men who had been his friends and benefactors make sorry reading. Small wonder that Prince Lobkowitz wrote to the Archduke that he had ' reason to be anything but satisfied with the behaviour of Beethoven towards me ', and it is to his undying credit that he remained Beethoven's friend and supporter until his own death in 1816.

Another instance of Beethoven's lack of ordinary judgment was his interference in the affairs of his brother Johann, who, having set up in business as an apothecary in Linz, was living with his housekeeper Therese Obermeyer. Beethoven travelled to Linz in October 1812 in order to persuade his brother to give up the liaison, and when protests and arguments had no effect, obtained a police injunction ordering Therese to leave the town. Johann promptly and predictably married her. It was against this background of sordid family strife that the eighth symphony was composed; the seventh had been completed earlier in the year, and in December the serene violin sonata op 96 was played for the first time by Rode, for whom it was written.

THE 'BATTLE SYMPHONY' AND THE CONGRESS OF VIENNA

It was about this time that Beethoven struck up a friendship with Johann Nepomuk Maelzel, a pianist with an overpoweringly inventive turn of mind, who was busy devising an instrument for fixing the exact tempo of music by a mechanically recurring beat. His first idea was a device with hammer and anvil, which he called the ' chronometer '; the metronome, with its pendulum principle, he invented a year or so later. When he asked Beethoven to mark his music by the metronome, the composer at first declared ' It is silly stuff, one must feel the tempo ', but later provided certain of his works with metronome marks which to this day give rise to controversy among scholars and conductors. The scope of Maelzel's inventiveness ranged from ear trumpets to help Beethoven's deafness to a mechanical brass band, operated by rotating cylinders with pins, which he named the ' Panharmonicon ' and which performed music by Handel and Cherubini. The two men conceived the plan of taking this machine to England and capturing the ears of the London public by means of a piece which Beethoven was to write for it, the ' Battle symphony ' (as its London publisher called it in 1816), celebrating Wellington's latest victory over Napoleon's armies in Spain. Then, to secure publicity and the funds to finance the trip, they planned first to collaborate in a charity concert in aid of wounded soldiers and for which Beethoven was to produce a fully orchestral version of the ' Battle symphony ', and then to follow this up with further concerts given for profit. The charity concert was a wild success. All the leading musicians of Vienna took part, Beethoven became overnight a popular composer in every sense of the word, and the seventh symphony (which had been included in the programme for good measure) rode to recognition in the wake of the preposterous 'Battle symphony'.

The projected benefit concerts followed and were equally successful. But by now Beethoven was involved in a revision of *Fidelio* for a projected revival and was reluctant to leave Vienna for the English venture. The unfortunate Maelzel, having tried in vain to secure some legal rights to the orchestral version (the mechanical version was indisputably his) had the parts copied surreptitiously and produced the piece in Munich. Beethoven instituted legal proceedings which dragged on for several years, until in 1817 the two men made up the quarrel and agreed to share the costs.

Napoleon's defeat at Leipzig and exile to Elba was followed in the autumn of 1814 by the gathering of Europe's sovereigns and statesmen in Vienna for the congress that was to celebrate Europe's liberation and ensure a lasting peace. No-one who has lived through the end of two world wars in our own century can fail to understand the relief, the jubilation, the uprush of loyalty and affection towards the assembled potentates, an affection which the subsequent period of deadening reaction was so little to justify. At Count Rasoumofsky's palace and in the apartments of the Archduke Rudolph, Beethoven was presented to the Emperor and Empress of Russia and other sovereigns who vied with each other to do him honour. The revised *Fidelio* was twice successfully performed, and a concert of his works at the imperial palace once more presented the 'Battle symphony' in double harness with the seventh symphony, together with a topical cantata, *Der glorreiche Augenblick* ('The glorious moment'). The glory was shortlived. In December Rasoumofsky's splendid palace was burned down; the fire had started in a temporary hall which he had erected for his vast receptions, and his losses were so great that he was forced to disband his quartet. Early in 1815 Napoleon escaped from Elba, and the concluding stages of the congress were hurried through under the threat of further war.

Financially Beethoven was now in a better position. He had received valuable presents from the great personages attending the congress, besides the profits from his concerts, and legal settlements had been reached regarding his annuities. He had valuable contacts with a new Viennese publisher, Steiner & Company, through its able young manager Tobias Haslinger, and also with London, where his old pupil Ferdinand Ries had now made his home. Ferdinand Ries now secured him a commission from the recently founded Philharmonic Society for three concert overtures, for which he received £75. This he met, not by composing new works, as had been expected, but by sending three already extant, the *Name day,* the *Ruins of Athens* and *King Stephen,* all uninspired occasional compositions. This undoubtedly cost him further valuable commissions, and makes the continuing friendliness and generosity of the Philharmonic Society towards him all the more honourable.

BROTHER AND NEPHEW

Notwithstanding his comparative prosperity he was still anxious about money, chiefly on account of his brother Caspar Carl, who for the past two years had been ill with tuberculosis. Caspar Carl's earlier attempts to manage his elder brother's business affairs had proved a failure and a source of disagreement, and his marriage had driven them still further apart, for his wife Johanna Reiss was a woman of tarnished reputation; their child Karl was in fact born only four months after their marriage. But now Beethoven, with the collapse of his hopes and longings for marriage and a family, swung once more towards his brother, whom he helped with money and surrounded with an almost excessive solicitude, and fastened his starved affections on the boy Karl, then a lively child of nine. It was thus natural that Caspar Carl, as his health rapidly failed, should think of appointing Ludwig as guardian to his son in the event of his own death. This he did by will, but added a codicil declaring that Karl was to remain with his mother.

This was the prologue to a tragedy: for Beethoven himself, for the widowed mother, and for Karl. Beethoven, convinced to the point of obsession that Johanna was a ' bad woman ' and unfit to have charge of her son, fought for the custody of the child through successive courts for five years. Meanwhile he took him from his mother and first placed him in a good boarding school, of which the head, Giannatasio del Rio, and his wife and daughters, were his friends and admirers. He then took him away and tried to make a home for him in his own chaotic household, turning for help and advice in this wholly unaccustomed task to his old and faithful friends Andreas and Nanette Streicher, who had tried on previous occasions to bring some sort of order into his surroundings. His consuming anxiety was to keep Karl from seeing his mother; hers, understandably, was to see her only child as often as possible. ' Karl has done wrong, but—a mother—a mother—even a bad mother is still a mother ', wrote Beethoven to Nanette Streicher after discovering that Johanna had been bribing the servants into letting her see her son. Despite this solitary flash of insight he remained totally unaware of the damage being inflicted on Karl by the forcible separation from his mother, by the ensuing conflict of loyalties, and by his own alternations of harshness and devouring affection. When, a little later, Karl ran away to his mother, it caused Beethoven untold anguish and anxiety and seemed to him a sign of moral obliquity. But a far greater obliquity was being formed upon the child as he inevitably developed habits of concealment and untruthfulness and let himself be cajoled into calling his mother evil names to please his uncle.

It was a harassing and depressing time for Beethoven, what with the protracted legal action over the guardianship of Karl, and continued troubles, mostly of his own making, over his domestic arrangements and the boy's schooling. He was frequently unwell, and his hearing was deteriorating. Up till 1816 he had been able, with mechanical aids, to hear his own playing, but by 1817 Czerny states that he could no longer hear music, and by 1818 his hearing was too poor for normal conversation, even with an ear trumpet. From then on his friends were driven to converse with him by means of notebooks which he kept for the purpose. These conversation books, of which just over 400 have been preserved, are like a one-sided telephone conversation, for his own replies, naturally, do not appear save in the rare cases where the discussion occurred in a public place and he preferred to write down his answers.

In June 1817 a warm-hearted letter from Ferdinand Ries brought him an invitation from the Philharmonic Society to visit London in the following winter season; he was to compose and direct the performance of two symphonies for the society, at a fee of three hundred guineas, with the prospect of further commissions and concerts for his own benefit. After a certain amount of haggling Beethoven accepted the invitation and the generous terms offered. But the irresolution that was so strange and incongruous an element in his nature held him back, as did his preoccupation with Karl's schooling and his ill-judged project of taking him away from boarding school once more and making a home for him. And he could not nerve himself to begin work on the two symphonies for the Philharmonic Society. ' To begin a big work makes me shudder ', he once declared, and in fact since 1812, the year of the seventh and eighth symphonies, he had written few outstanding works, apart from the final revision of *Fidelio*: two piano sonatas, two cello sonatas and the song cycle *An die ferne Geliebte*. No doubt the worry and litigation over the custody of Karl had something to do with this. But the inner rhythm of an artist's life is independent of external events, and the arid wilderness through which he was passing lay in the realm of the spirit, though anxieties and growing isolation may have helped to lead him thither. In any case, a new conception had begun to take possession of him in these grey years from 1816 to 1818—the vast sonata in B flat, op 106, known as the *Hammerklavier*, which drew to itself all Beethoven's vitality, so that there was nothing left, just then, for the Philharmonic Society's symphonies. Thus, in spite of continued half-made plans and the happy stimulus of the Broadwood piano sent to him as a gift by the head of the firm, he let slip the opportunity of a visit to London, with all the artistic and material rewards and human encouragement it might have brought. Not that he ever formally abandoned the project, for he went on thinking and corresponding about it; and in fact, it touched off the creative process that, in the next six years, produced the ninth symphony.

Throughout 1819 litigation continued over the guardianship and

41

education of Karl. At one point the case was transferred from one court to another, since it emerged that Beethoven (despite the 'van' in his name) was not of noble birth, so that the Vienna City Court, which had jurisdiction over commoners, ought by rights to be trying the case. Again it dragged on, with Karl sent from one school to another; the guardianship was awarded first to Beethoven, with a member of the court as joint guardian, then to Johanna, also with a co-guardian. Beethoven then took the case on appeal to a higher court, but it was not until 1820 that it was finally decided in his favour, with himself and a friend, a tutor in the Lobkowitz household, as joint guardians. Karl meanwhile was at boarding school, doing rather badly: not surprisingly, since the stability and sense of security which are essential to any child's healthy development had not been his for the past five years.

Early in 1819 Beethoven learned that the Archduke Rudolph, who, like so many princely younger sons, had entered the church, was to be enthroned as archbishop of Olmütz. The news prompted him to embark on a mass for the occasion. Although he had cut adrift from Catholic orthodoxy, he was—in the phrase applied to the equally unorthodox Jew Spinoza—a 'God-intoxicated' man, and the project took complete possession of him. For four years —the celebration for which the mass was intended long past—he worked on it, restudying the all too familiar text in translation and going back to what he called 'the church chorales of the monks' (in fact, a profoundly intuitive exploration of the potentialities of sixteenth century modal harmony). Towards the end of 1819, worried about money, he was driven to ask his publisher Steiner for a loan, and in 1820, still wrestling with the mass, the evolving ninth symphony and three piano sonatas, he borrowed again, this time from his old friend Franz Brentano. One of the sonatas, the E major op 109, was dedicated in gratitude to Brentano's daughter. He had in 1819 invested the money presented to him during the Congress of Vienna, four thousand florins, in eight bank shares; but these he regarded as Karl's patrimony and refused to draw on them to meet his daily needs. The year 1821 was one of incessant work and recurring illness, and it was not until 1822 that the mass was finished, and, in its wake, the last two piano sonatas.

With the publication of the mass in prospect, Beethoven set in motion a tortuous correspondence with half a dozen publishers at once, to each of whom, at one time or another, he promised exclusive rights in the work: his old friend Simrock in Bonn, Schlesinger in Berlin, Peters in Leipzig and Schott in Mainz, as well as his two main publishers in Vienna, Steiner and Artaria. At this epoch, when the law of copyright was still in its infancy, music publishers often brought out pirated editions of works for which they had not paid, and relations between publisher and composer were often largely a battle of wits. But even when this is realised, the readiness of Beethoven's prospective publishers to trust his word and advance him money, and his own blend of fine phrases and double dealing, make sorry reading. He was in fact still in financial difficulties; for this reason he also devised the expedient of writing round to various European sovereigns soliciting subscriptions for manuscript copies of the mass at fifty ducats each; he only got ten subscribers. In the end he brought himself to sell one of the bank shares he had set aside for Karl, and paid off most of his debts. He then appointed Karl his legal heir.

In the autumn of 1822 *Fidelio* was revived, and the youthful Wilhelmine Schroeder-Devrient, as Leonora, gave an inspired performance. This should have been a joyful event for Beethoven, who was to have directed the production, but it was turned to bitterness for him because his deafness made it impossible for him to conduct. The young Anton Schindler, a law student turned musician, who from about 1819 onwards had become Beethoven's devoted unpaid secretary and general factotum, has described the breakdown of the rehearsal, at which nobody had the heart to tell Beethoven what was wrong, until Beethoven handed his conversation pad to Schindler with an unspoken query which Schindler answered by writing merely ' Please do not go on, more at home '. As if he had been struck Beethoven turned and fled from the theatre. One outcome of this was a last despairing bout of medical consultation and treatment, but nothing could be done.

THE NINTH SYMPHONY

London was still in his thoughts. He had asked Ferdinand Ries about the possibility of the Philharmonic Society commissioning a symphony from him, and Ries's reply that they would offer fifty pounds at last precipitated the work on the ninth symphony that had been going on in the margin of his mind for years; as he worked at it through the summer of 1823 he came to think of it as the 'symphony for England'. It was about this time that he received from a Russian nobleman, Prince Nicholas Galitzin, a commission for three string quartets. This brought into full activity ideas that were already stirring at the back of his mind, completely displacing his plans for an opera on a libretto by the Viennese poet Grillparzer, and also his halfhearted negotiations about an oratorio commissioned by the Gesellschaft der Musikfreunde (the Viennese counterpart of London's Philharmonic Society), who generously let the matter drop without attempting to recover the money they had already advanced.

It is important to realise that by now Beethoven, in his early fifties, was regarded throughout Europe as the greatest composer living. Vienna, it is true, was in the grip of that 'Rossini fever' which swept the continent as one captivating opera after another flowed from the brilliant and still youthful composer, and Beethoven (who after all had been outwardly a dormant volcano for some years) was apparently neglected by the public. But the generosity of the Gesellschaft der Musikfreunde over the oratorio testifies to the regard in which he was held, and while his eccentricities were already a legend, his outspoken comments on public affairs were ignored or tolerated, even in the stifling atmosphere of the inefficient police state that had succeeded the buoyant hopefulness and good-will of the brief congress epoch. And from every European country pilgrims sought him out. Charles Neate and Cipriani Potter, Sir John Russell and Johann Andreas Stumpff, Edward Schultz and Sir George Smart all came from London, and have left graphic accounts of their encounters with him; his reception of them, though occasionally forbidding, seems more often to have surprised them by its geniality. Liszt, as a prodigy of eleven, was brought by his teacher Czerny to play to Beethoven, and Beethoven actually invited Weber to call on him, greeted him with embraces and called him 'a devil of a fellow'. Rossini himself called to pay his respects, and, so far from resenting being bluntly told to confine himself to *opera buffa*, was so moved with pity and positive embarrassment at the contrast between his own dazzling success and the neglect of Beethoven that he tried to raise an annuity fund for him, only to be told that he was impossible to help—' a misanthrope, cranky and can't keep friends '.

For all that, when it became known in 1824 that he was considering the possibility of taking his new symphony to Berlin for its first performance, a group of his admirers headed by Count Moritz Lichnowsky (brother of his old friend and patron) addressed to him a petition begging him to give the work in Vienna. Touched and heartened, he agreed, and after endless delays and difficulties, almost all due to his inability to make up his mind on either musical or business matters, the concert finally took place at the Kärntnerthor theatre in May 1824. The programme consisted of the overture *The consecration of the house*, three sections of the Mass in D (labelled ' three Grand Hymns ' to meet the objections of the authorities to performing liturgical music in a theatre) and the ninth symphony. Schuppanzigh led the orchestra and Umlauf, who had directed the 1822 revival of *Fidelio*, was conductor; Beethoven, nominally ' participating in the direction ', was on the podium, but Umlauf, taught by past experience, told the orchestra to ignore Beethoven's beat and follow his. The audience was wildly enthusiastic, but it was not until the young contralto soloist Caroline Unger had taken him gently by the sleeve and turned him round to face the auditorium that Beethoven became aware of the applause.

Unfortunately, despite a full house, the financial result of the concert was far less than Beethoven had expected, owing to the heavy expenses involved. He became convinced that he had been cheated and, having invited Schuppanzigh, Umlauf and the long-suffering Schindler to dine with him, burst out with accusations that they had swindled him. Unable to convince him of the injustice of his accusations, they left, leaving him and his nephew to finish the supposedly festive meal alone.

At the end of 1824 the patient and persistent Philharmonic Society had again sent Beethoven, through Charles Neate, an invitation to visit London. The ninth symphony was about to be rehearsed and they hoped that Beethoven would be able to conduct it in person at the first concert of their season in January 1825. Once more he thought of it with eagerness, haggled, hesitated while his friends urged him to take the plunge, both for the sake of his health and of his financial situation. In the end he wrote postponing his journey till the autumn. In March the ninth symphony received its first London performance without him and there was no more talk of a visit.

One reason for his inability to make up his mind about the London visit was undoubtedly that his energies were now entirely absorbed by the quartets for Prince Nicholas Galitzin. The one in E flat major, op 127, had been sent off to the prince at the end of 1824 and was first performed in Vienna in March 1825.

The composition of the other two quartets was interrupted by illness, an inflammation of the bowels, which kept him indoors for a month. For once his doctor of the moment, Braunhofer, succeeded in gaining his confidence and making him stick to the treatment and diet he prescribed. During his convalescence Beethoven worked at the A minor quartet op 132, the central movement of which is headed ' Heiliger Dankgesang eines Genesenen an die Gottheit . .' (Holy song of thanksgiving to the Godhead from one recovered from illness.) It was finished in August, and by November he had completed the third of the set, op 130 in B flat, and the A minor had received its first performance, this time with Schuppanzigh as leader.

KARL'S ATTEMPT AT SUICIDE
Karl was now nearly nineteen, and studying philology at the university. Beethoven made the mistake that many lesser men have made in regard to their children—that of overestimating the boy's intellect and trying to force him into an ideal mould, instead of allowing him to follow his natural bent. Karl was not the genius that Beethoven thought him, but (in Alan Tyson's felicitous phrase) ' a rather decent and patient adolescent ', who wanted to enter the army, and put his wish to his uncle reasonably and modestly. Beethoven disapproved and would not hear of it, but early in 1825 he allowed Karl to leave the university and enter the polytechnic institute to train for a business career.

At first all seemed to be going well, but as the year went on tension increased between Karl and his uncle. Karl was now living in lodgings and yearning for independence, but Beethoven could not let him alone. During his long summer convalescence in Baden he bombarded Karl with letters, errands and demands for visits, and after he had returned to Vienna he tried to keep a watch on him, hung about the institute to take him home or visited him and made violent scenes in his rooms. It was in vain that a recent friend of Beethoven's, a young civil servant and amateur violinist named Karl Holz, tried to bridge the widening chasm between them by winning Karl's friendship and confidence and going about with him. Holz did what he could to reassure Beethoven about the boy's habits and persuade him to allow him more money, for Beethoven kept him on such a tight rein that he was driven to borrow from the servants. Beethoven's letters to Karl, full of alternating reproaches and passionate tenderness and forgiveness, are heartrending to read. But Karl's entries in Beethoven's conversation books, replying to cross-questioning about money or standing up for a friend of his of whom Beethoven disapproved, are hardly less painful. There is a terrible bitterness, too, in the note he wrote to his friend, ' I had to write to you in such a hurry from fear and worry of being discovered by the old fool ': so completely had Beethoven lost his love and respect. The lad clearly felt trapped—by constant surveil- lance, by impending examinations, by having run into debt. At the end of July he ran away, bought pistols and ammunition, drove out into the country, and in the Helenenthal, the valley where he and his uncle had often taken their summer walks, discharged both pistols at his head.

He only succeeded in wounding himself, and a passing carter found him and took him to his mother, who sent for Beethoven. The shock and grief to him were indescribable; Stephan von Breuning's son Gerhard, then a little boy, records that his mother 'met him on the glacis, completely undone '. Characteristically, the Breunings asked him to come to them for all meals so that he would not be alone. Karl was taken to hospital, and the inevitable police inquiries brought more pain, for Karl stated bluntly that he had shot himself because his uncle ' tormented him too much ', adding ' I grew worse because my uncle wanted me to be better '. As he mended, consultations took place at his bedside and among Beethoven's friends regarding his future. He reiterated his wish to enter the army and, with the support of Breuning and Schindler, carried the day. Breuning, who had gallantly undertaken the guardianship which Beethoven had at last been persuaded to relinquish, arranged for him to be accepted as a cadet, as soon as he was well enough, in a regiment commanded by a certain Baron von Stutterheim. For giving Karl a helping hand this officer was rewarded by the dedication of the C sharp minor quartet.

The intervening time, until Karl was completely recovered, presented problems, as Beethoven was desperately anxious that he should not go to his mother. An invitation from Beethoven's brother Johann, who a few years earlier had bought himself a country property, offered a solution, and by the end of September uncle and nephew were installed at Gneixendorf. They settled down to some sort of routine, and it was here that Beethoven composed his last string quartet, op 135 in F major, and also the new last movement which he had been persuaded to provide for the B flat quartet op 130 to replace the vast and intractable fugal finale, which was then published separately. But he was again unwell, with symptoms of liver trouble, and tension again began to mount between him and Karl, who was otherwise quite enjoying the life. Towards the end of November 1826, Johann, who according to his lights had tried to make the visit a success, felt it his duty to write his brother a letter pointing out that it was high time that Karl took steps to join his regiment, and that the longer he delayed the harder it would be for him. It was sensible advice, and in the following week, probably on December 1, Beethoven and Karl set out for Vienna.

LAST ILLNESS
They travelled in an open carriage, since Johann's closed carriage had taken his wife to Vienna the week before (the story that Johann refused it to his brother is probably untrue). At their overnight lodging, in an unheated bedroom, Beethoven developed a hacking cough, and reached Vienna the next day with pneumonia. A note was sent to Holz, and he and Karl between them sent round to

various doctors. (Another myth, probably originating in Schindler's antipathy to Karl, is that he neglected his uncle for billiards; in fact the conversation books show that he was with him almost daily, in the intervals of medical examinations and other preliminaries, until, early in January, he left for his regiment.) In the end they secured Dr Wawruch from the General Hospital, who succeeded in bringing down Beethoven's temperature, and by December 7 he was well enough to write a long letter to his old and cherished friends the Wegelers in Bonn.

It was all the more of a shock to Dr Wawruch to find him, a few days later, in the throes of a violent attack of diarrhoea and jaundiced all over his body. Dropsy developed, and two successive tapping operations brought only temporary relief. Beethoven began to lose patience, and sent Schindler to his old friend Dr Malfatti (uncle of the girl he had wanted to marry sixteen years before) and begged him to come. After some professional and personal hesitation Malfatti came, and prescribed frozen punch, which at first seemed to work wonders; Beethoven slept well, sweated profusely, felt greatly refreshed and began to feel the urge to work again. But again, the improvement was only shortlived, and by March it was apparent that he was not responding to treatment and that the end could only be a matter of time.

Friends did all they could for him. Schindler was there almost daily, and so was the boy Gerhard von Breuning, bringing books and insect powder and keeping Beethoven amused by his gay and solicitous chatter. Old friends like Gleichenstein and Count Moritz Lichnowsky, and Schuppanzigh with his team, came to visit him, Schubert came with Anselm Hüttenbrenner to pay his respects, and old Zmeskall, crippled and bedridden, wrote to ask after him and received an affectionate reply.

Two years earlier, a German harp maker living, in London, Johann Andreas Stumpff, had visited him and heard him declare that Handel was the greatest composer who ever lived, but that a poor devil like himself could not afford the scores of his works. Stumpff vowed then and there to make him a present of them, and in December there had arrived from him the forty volumes of Handel's complete works, in Arnold's edition. Beethoven was overjoyed at the ' royal ' gift, as he called it, and got little Gerhard von Breuning to bring the big volumes over to his bed one by one. In February he wrote to thank Stumpff and asked him at the same time if it would be possible for the Philharmonic Society to give a concert for his benefit, as his illness had brought heavy expenses and made it impossible for him to earn. Stumpff and the society acted quickly, and on February 28 £100 was voted ' to be sent through the hands of Mr Moscheles to some confidential friend of Beethoven, to be applied to his comforts and necessities during his illness '. The money arrived in the middle of March and was received with relief and gratitude.

It was about this time that Dr Wawruch told him in writing that he was going to die, ' so that he might do his duty as a citizen and to religion '. Beethoven received this communication, Wawruch added, ' with unexampled composure '. With the help of his friends, and with great physical effort, he made and signed his will, in which he named Karl his sole heir, and also signed the formal transfer of the guardianship to Stephan von Breuning. Wawruch, his brother Johann and his despised sister in law Therese asked him to receive the last sacraments, to which he replied, quietly and firmly, ' I wish it '. Schindler, Breuning and his sister in law were present when the viaticum was brought to him, and heard him thank the priest for ' this last service '. On March 24 he went into a coma and lay for two days unconscious, with his friends coming and going around him. The end came on the afternoon of March 26 1827.

Vast crowds watched the funeral and followed the procession to the cemetery, where a moving oration written by Grillparzer was spoken by the great tragedian Anschutz; the most distinguished musicians in the city, Schubert among them, were pallbearers or torchbearers. Nobody was in any doubt that they were laying to rest the greatest composer of the age.

Books in English about Beethoven

LETTERS, CONVERSATION BOOKS AND NOTEBOOKS: Although Beethoven was a copious letter writer he was, as J W N Sullivan observed, 'exceptionally insensitive to language'. Yet it is hard to understand W H Auden's statement that he had found only one memorable sentence among all his letters, so forcefully and with such raw immediacy do they reflect his preoccupations, whether love or business, friendships or quarrels, money or health. A complete edition, *The letters of Beethoven,* translated and edited by Emily Anderson, appeared in 1961 (Macmillan, three volumes). This is a work of immense and patient scholarship, based on personal study of the autographs and involving the decipherment of Beethoven's handwriting, wellnigh unintelligible, in his later years, to all but the expert. Footnotes provide the necessary biographical details about the recipients of the letters and the events reflected in them. Miss Anderson described the aim of her translation as 'a sort of timeless English', which in practice produces a certain flatness. A paperback, *Selected letters of Beethoven* (Macmillan, 1967) containing some 180 of the letters out of a total of close on 1600 in the complete edition, has been edited by Alan Tyson, with revised footnotes and an excellent introduction.

Until Emily Anderson's translation appeared, the only available edition of Beethoven's letters in English was J S Shedlock's two volume selection from A C Kalischer's German edition of 1907-8; this appeared in 1909 (Dent). Two American publications did something to span the gap: O G Sonneck's *Beethoven letters in America* (NY, Beethoven Association; Hawkes, 1927), containing thirty five letters with facsimiles and explanatory notes, and *New Beethoven letters,* translated and annotated by Donald W MacArdle and Ludwig Misch (University of Oklahoma Press, 1957). This does not claim to present previously unpublished material: its object was to provide an English version of all the letters that had been brought to light since the appearance of Shedlock's two volumes. Where the authors were unable to study the autographs they worked from the published sources in German. Their translations, more elliptical than Miss Anderson's, are very readable; the annotations give the printed source for each letter, and much scholarly background material. The book appeared just too soon to include the recently discovered letters from Beethoven to Josephine Deym, published in the same year by the *Beethovenhaus* in Bonn.

Beethoven's conversation books have not been translated into English, but Donald W MacArdle, in his *Index to Beethoven's conversation books* (' Detroit studies in music bibliography ' no 3, 1962) describes them and gives an account of the editions brought out by Nohl (1924), Schünemann (1941-3) and Prod'homme (1946, in French). The index, which covers the three editions, is almost entirely of persons and makes no reference to Beethoven's works.

In addition to the letters and conversation books, Beethoven kept various notebooks in which he made diary entries and other memoranda. Extracts from these were copied, along with a quantity of letters and other material formerly in the possession of young Karl van Beethoven, by his mother's legal adviser Jakob Hotschevar. The originals are now lost or dispersed; the copy, bought by the Berlin Library in 1959, is known by the name of a previous owner as the ' Fischoff manuscript '. This is the source of those diary entries quoted by Thayer and later biographers, which disclose, often most movingly, Beethoven's states of mind. It is also drawn on by Michael Hamburger in his *Beethoven: letters, journals and conversations* (Cape 1951, 1961, *pb* 1966). This is a composite picture derived, as the title implies, from conversation books and notebooks as well as correspondence, and also to some extent from other people's memories. A vivid portrait emerges, much more revealing and complete than letters alone could give. There is a well written and perceptive introduction but it is unfortunate that there is no bibliography, for the book would be of greater value if the sources were listed and explained. An earlier compilation by Friedrich Kerst, *Beethoven the man and the artist, as revealed in his own words*, translated by H E Krehbiel (Gay and Bird 1906; London and NY, Bles, 1926, 1964), consists of short extracts from Beethoven's letters, journals and conversation books arranged under subject headings, but is too scrappy to be really useful. From a different angle, another composite picture of Beethoven as his pupils, visitors, friends and early biographers saw him is given by O G Sonneck in *Beethoven: impressions by his contemporaries* (NY, Schirmer, 1926; OUP, 1927; *pb* NY, Dover, 1967). It is admirably presented, with a short note on each contribution and its author.

GENERAL AND CRITICAL BIOGRAPHIES

The earliest full-scale biography of Beethoven is that undertaken by his devoted factotum Anton Felix Schindler. It was first published in 1840; an English translation and adaptation by Ignaz Moscheles appeared in 1841. In 1860 Schindler rewrote it completely, and this later version is now available in an excellent translation by Constance S Jolly, edited and annotated by Donald W MacArdle, under the title *Beethoven as I knew him* (Faber, 1966). The editing is essential. Schindler served Beethoven with a doglike, humourless devotion that can be, and in this case clearly was, on occasion, supremely irritating to its object. He aims at truthfulness, but finds it impossible to be fair to those who, in his eyes, wronged Beethoven or, worse, supplanted himself in the composer's regard. It is, moreover, a confusing, badly arranged book, more like a collection of materials for a biography than a finished work. Yet it is an essential source book, both from its human side and as a reflection of the social and musical mentality of the period. Schindler's record of Beethoven's opinions and pronouncements on musical matters, especially on metronome markings and on tempo in general, and his own comments on the performance of Beethoven's music, provide valuable material for the serious student.

The standard work on Beethoven's life, and one of the great biographical achievements of the nineteenth century, is the book by the American Alexander Wheelock Thayer, now reissued under the title *Thayer's life of Beethoven* (Princeton University Press,

1964). Yet it has had a chequered and confusing history, from the publication of its first two volumes (all that Thayer completed) in a German translation, its successive revisions and completion by other hands, its appearance in English in 1921, translated and further revised by H E Krehbiel; its latest edition has been prepared by Elliot Forbes, with further revisions, additions and notes embodying the results of the latest research, and the deletion of some obsolete material. Among Thayer's imperishable achievements was the collection of a vast amount of detailed material, by the most painstaking research, realising as he did that background history is an important aid to understanding; his account of the court music and musicians at Bonn through the eighteenth century is invaluable. Even more remarkable is his scrupulous honesty in presenting Beethoven truthfully, facing and presenting the more discreditable facts about his conduct, in defiance of the heroic image built up in the last century by those who could not believe that the man could be less noble than the music. His subsequent editors have aimed at a like truthfulness. The book is a strictly factual record, with no discussion of Beethoven's music, and is pedestrian in style; but it is an essential foundation and working tool for the student, and Professor Forbes's edition has now made it accessible and up to date, though a word of caution is needed about certain misprints and inaccuracies, especially over publication dates.

Among the earliest studies of Beethoven's life and work produced in England was the long essay written by Sir George Grove for the first edition of his *Dictionary of music*, published in 1878-90. When the fifth edition (1954) was being prepared, its editor, Eric Blom, came to the conclusion that this, with two more of Grove's original essays, should be replaced as being out of scale and in some respects out of date, but that their value was so great as to warrant their preservation in a separate reprint. This appeared under the title *Beethoven, Schubert, Mendelssohn* (Macmillan, 1951); Eric Blom provided an introduction and made such corrections as were needed. The Beethoven essay is solidly based on Thayer and on Grove's own intensive studies, and has penetrating things to say, as for example, of the composer's use of fugue, that 'nothing in the whole of Beethoven's music is associated with a more distinct dramatic intention '. It may fittingly be added here that the essay by W G McNaught which replaced that by Grove in the 1954 edition of the dictionary is a splendid picture, compassionate yet clearheaded, of both man and musician.

Daniel Gregory Mason's *Beethoven and his forerunners* (Macmillan 1904, revised 1930), a youthful work by a distinguished American composer and lecturer, is completely dated, even with the bibliographical material added to the 1930 edition.

Mason's excellent book on the string quartets, mentioned later (p 64) is in a different class altogether. A curious case is Romain Rolland's little *Beethoven* of 1903 (Drane, 1907, translated by F Rothwell; Kegan Paul's ' Library of music and musicians ', 1917, translated by B Constance Hull, with additional musical analyses by A Eaglefield Hull). Read in cold blood it can only be described as slight, unscholarly and hopelessly over-emotional. But in the light of Leo Schrade's ponderous but thought-provoking *Beethoven in France: the growth of an idea* (Yale University Press, 1942) it reveals itself as a landmark in French musical thought, a rallying point for those who were working for France's regeneration from the decadence and pessimism of the *fin de siècle,* and the bible of a new religion of Beethoven as the prophet and exemplar of redemption through suffering. In this context Vincent D'Indy's *Beethoven: a critical biography,* translated by Theodore Baker (NY, Schirmer, 1911) is seen as a counterblast to this movement from the standpoint of orthodox religion, which explains its excessive concern to demonstrate Beethoven's ' Christian and Catholic ' outlook. D'Indy is indeed unreliable as a historian, but he had a composer's insight into the creative mind of another, and the best of this book finds its way into the essay he contributed to Cobbett's *Cyclopedic survey of chamber music* (see below, p 65).

Continuing the line of French studies, André de Hévesy's *Beethoven the man,* a translation by F S Flint of *Beethoven. Vie intime* (Faber and Gwyer, 1927) examines Beethoven's relations with the Brunsvik family, and contains interesting documents and research about them and other friends of Beethoven including Countess Marie Erdödy. Somewhat sketchy and superficial in approach, it has been largely superseded by Romain Rolland's extended study of Beethoven, of which the first part, *Beethoven the creator: from the Eroica to the Appassionata,* was translated by Ernest Newman (Gollancz, 1929; NY, Dover, *pb* 1964). Rolland was not primarily a musicologist but a creative artist in his own right, an author and man of letters and a student of European literature. Hence his discussion of the music, though it springs from real knowledge and understanding, tends too much to subjective interpretation; characteristically, the finest chapter is on *Fidelio* and its roots in French opera under the influence of the Revolution. The appendices are important. The first propounds a theory of his deafness, much disputed, that it was caused by the very intensity of his inner concentration. (On this subject the little monograph by Dr Maurice Sorsby, *Beethoven's deafness,* an offprint from the *Journal of laryngology and otology,* August 1930, anticipates later diagnoses of nerve deafness, possibly connected with his chronic intestinal troubles.) Another appendix, devoted to the Brunsvik family, is based on Therese's diaries and other family papers, and gives a wonderful account of Therese and her mental and spiritual development. A revealing postscript is provided by Rolland's *Goethe and Beethoven,* translated by G A Pfister and E S Kemp (NY, Harper; Hamish Hamilton, 1931); this consists of four separate essays on the contacts between the two men, on Goethe himself and on Bettina Brentano. In the same tradition, Edouard Herriot's *The life and times of Beethoven,* translated by A I and W J Mitchell (Macmillan, 1935) is a very personal and very French interpretation, by a distinguished statesman and man of letters, of Beethoven's personality and art. Its chief value lies in its assessment of what Napoleon, in idea and in fact, stood for in Beethoven's development, and in its discussion of the writers who influenced Beethoven and those who in their turn were influenced by him; it is the more unfortunate that there is no bibliography.

Among the best short biographies is Harvey Grace's *Ludwig van Beethoven* (' Masters of music ' series. Kegan Paul, Curwen, 1927); his account of Beethoven's life is admirable in its dispassionate sympathy. The essay on the music, an addition to the original plan of the book, is enlightening despite its compression. Robert Haven Schauffler's *Beethoven, the man who freed music* (Curtis Brown,

1929; NY, Doubleday Doran, 1937) is an odd mixture of sane humanity, faulty history and turgid style. Musically, his discussion of Beethoven's use of 'germ' and 'source' motives makes valid points, though he tends to find them in impossible places.

Madeleine Goss's *Beethoven: master musician* (NY, Doubleday Doran, 1931; revised edition Henry Holt, 1946) is a fictionalised biography, the best feature of which is the table 'The world that Beethoven lived in', setting out his life, musical happenings and world events in parallel columns. Alan Pryce-Jones contributed the *Beethoven* volume to Duckworth's 'Great lives' series (1933, revised 1948, reprinted 1958); this is a short biography with no discussion of the music, written with somewhat unsympathetic acumen. Richard Specht's *Beethoven as he lived* (Macmillan, 1933) suffers from Alfred Kalisch's translation from an excessively emotional approach, and is unreliable as history, though there are flashes of real insight. Marion Scott's *Beethoven* was an outstanding addition to the 'Master musicians' series when it appeared in 1934 (Dent; NY, Dutton, last reprinted 1965). Marion Scott was a fine scholar and an experienced chamber music player, and a writer of keen intuitive understanding, both human and musical. While it is possible to feel that on the personal side her attitude is too emotionally involved, few would disagree with Tovey's judgment that she 'has dealt with the music in a manner which would be difficult to overpraise'.

In J N Burk's *The life and works of Beethoven* (NY, Random House, 1943) the biography is written with insight and great distinction. The musical section is less satisfactory, being in the nature of a catalogue of works incorporating a string of programme notes, sometimes excellent but omitting any discussion of a number of important compositions. Emil Ludwig's *Beethoven: life of a conqueror* (Hutchinson, London, 1943) shows considerable human understanding and, on the whole, does not falsify or oversimplify. His interpretations of the music are too subjective to be of value as serious analysis, and the translation, by G S McManus, contains some inaccuracies. Manuel Komroff's *Beethoven and the world of music* (NY, Dodd Mead, 1961) is unreliable both about the social and historical background and about the music, but is redeemed by

57

the sound sense it brings to bear on Beethoven the man and his human relationships.

Pictorial biographies are in a special category, for they present the composer, his friends, and the setting of their lives, through contemporary eyes. Erich Valentin's *Beethoven: a pictorial biography* (Thames and Hudson, 1958) and Robert Bory's *Ludwig van Beethoven: his life and work in pictures* (NY, Atlantis Books, 1960; Thames and Hudson, 1966) are both outstanding. In Valentin's book, translated from the German by Norman Deane, the biographical essay contains some misprints and inaccuracies, and tends to idealise its subject unduly, but the illustrations are admirably chosen, reproduced and documented. The biographical part of Bory's book is no more than a prefatory sketch, but the pictures carry on the story both by their grouping and their lucid captions, and comprise facsimilies of autographs and important documents as well as portraits and topographical prints. In a more popular style, *The life and times of Beethoven*, by Gino Pugnetti, translated by Laila Pauk (Hamyln, 'Portraits of greatness' series, 1967) shows real imagination in its choice of contemporary prints and portraits, and an astonishing lack of judgment in treating wholly imaginary mid nineteenth century narrative paintings on the same level. The documentation is minimal; in many cases even the artists' names are not given, and the biographical commentary is far from reliable.

Percy Young and Stanley Sadie have each contributed the *Beethoven* volume to a series of illustrated biographies with music examples, designed for young people. Percy Young's account (Ernest Benn, 'Masters of music' series, 1966) is well and attractively done, despite a few odd mistakes, and on the whole not unduly idealised. Stanley Sadie (Faber, 'The great composers', 1967) treats life and works in conjunction, with real understanding. The music examples are set out in short score for reading at the piano.

SPECIAL STUDIES

A group of specialised studies deals with single aspects of the composer's life. Such are J Mewburn Levien's *Beethoven and the Philharmonic Society* (Novello, 1927), and Ernest Closson's *L'élément flamand dans Beethoven,* a study of Beethoven's Flemish ancestry and its influence on his temperament and his music, which appeared in 1936 under the title *The Fleming in Beethoven* (OUP), translated by Muriel Fuller. O G Sonneck in *The riddle of the immortal beloved* (NY, Schirmer, 1927) sums up the conflicting evidence and concludes that her identity is unknown and likely to remain so. An attempt to claim the honour for Countess Marie Erdödy is made by Dana Steichen in *Beethoven's beloved,* a lengthy biographical study produced as a photostat of a typescript (copyright 1959 by Edward Steichen, Ridgefield, Connecticut). Much of the author's argument, based on interpretations and datings of letters, is invalidated by later findings as presented by Emily Anderson.

Beethoven and his nephew, by Edith and Richard Sterba, translated by Willard R Trask (NY, Pantheon, 1954; Dobson, 1957) is at once authoritative and highly controversial. The authors apply the principles and methods of Freudian psychoanalysis to the known facts and documents concerning Beethoven's family relationships. It makes enlightening, deeply depressing and not always convincing reading; the authors are so intent on the psychological case history that they appear to leave out of account the effects on Beethoven of constant physical ill health and the draining of vitality into the work of composition. The reader cannot help gaining from it, however, a greater understanding of a tragic situation and a sympathy for Karl tinged with admiration for the dignity with which, on occasion, he stood his ground.

A small but important group of books is that in which Beethoven's life and character and his development as a musician are made to interpret one another. They are difficult to classify, for the biographical element varies greatly in length and scope. Paul Bekker's *Beethoven* (Berlin, 1911) first appeared in this country in 1925, translated by M M Bozman (Dent: NY, Dutton, revised edition with bibliography 1927, last reprinted 1939). The biographical section is very short, though an appendix (out of date in one or two of its statements) contains a very full summary of Beethoven's life. In his study of the music Bekker starts out from the belief that music is capable of conveying not only experiences outside the range of expression in words, but also definite conceptions. This leads him at times into an excess of extramusical interpretation. His discussion of the piano works, on the other hand, relates the music, in an illuminating way, to Beethoven's own piano playing and the instruments on which he played. J W N Sullivan's *Beethoven. His spiritual development* (Cape, 1927; reprinted by New Library 1937, *pb* Allen & Unwin, 1968) maintains, more convincingly, that music springs from the composer's inner experience and awareness of reality and can communicate this in its own terms; in the light of this he traces Beethoven's growth through and beyond heroic defiance to the acceptance of suffering as an essential part of experience, as revealed in the works of his final period. Here he is at one with Burnett James, whose *Beethoven and human destiny* (Phoenix House, 1960) contains some acute musical observations, especially on the liberating effects of fugue and of modal harmony on his use of tonality in the late works, alongside others that are purely subjective.

W J Turner's *Beethoven: the search for reality* (Benn, 1927) is a biographical study by a writer who was at once a poet, a music critic and a student of the metaphysical basis of music. The book consists of a full and reasonably reliable biographical section based largely on Thayer, and an extraordinarily thoughtful and intuitive discussion of Beethoven's inner life as revealed in his musical development, marred by a tiresome habit of comparing other composers with Beethoven, invariably to their disadvantage.

Ernest Newman's *The unconscious Beethoven. A study in musical psychology* (Parsons, 1927) was reissued in 1968 by Gollancz, with an introduction by Neville Cardus, to mark the centenary of Newman's birth. It is a remarkable pioneer study, anticipating by a generation some aspects of the Sterbas book, though later writers have not been convinced, as Newman is, that Beethoven had syphilis. His discussion of Beethoven's creative processes, and in particular of the 'great sketches' outlining the exposition of the first movement of the 'Eroica' symphony, is enthralling. A minutely detailed analysis of the same movement, no less enthralling in its way, is contained in Walter Riezler's splendid *Beethoven,* which appeared in England in 1938 (E C Forrester), well translated by G D H Pidcock, with an introduction by Wilhelm Furtwängler. Riezler's approach springs from his 'deep conviction of the autonomy of music'. He sets out to do the one job that words can accomplish, 'reveal the purely musical facts', and does so with a power and insight in which Tovey is almost his only rival. The short biographical section, is more of an essay for one who has already done some reading than an introduction for the newcomer.

Lastly, Martin Cooper's *Beethoven. The last decade 1817-1827*, (OUP, 1970) is a book of outstanding value and originality of approach. It tells the story of Beethoven's last ten years in some detail, drawing on the immediate past, in his own life and in contemporary history, in order to show what kind of man he had become. It then analyses with keen insight, the works of those years, bringing into focus those characteristics which, in conjunction, constitute their distinctive style, and showing how life and music interacted on each other. In so doing Cooper throws fresh and often unexpected light on aspects of Beethoven which are usually ignored or taken for granted, as in his account of the contemporary religious situation, in Bonn and in Vienna, and its effect on Beethoven's mentality and on his approach to the Mass in D. A unique feature of the book is an appendix on Beethoven's medical history by Dr Edward Larkin, who reviews afresh all the available medical evidence and, in the light of present day knowledge, advances the suggestion that Beethoven's widely varied symptoms and illness were all manifestations of what is loosely termed an allergic condition. Indeed, the effects of Beethoven's physical health on both his character and his music are treated by both Cooper and Larkin with exceptional clarity and penetration.

GENERAL CRITICISM

Among general surveys of Beethoven's music one of the first, and one of the best, is that by Ernest Walker; his *Beethoven* appeared in 1905 as the third volume of a series of short monographs entitled 'The music of the masters', edited by Wakeling Dry (John Lane, The Bodley Head; NY, John Lane Company, reprinted

1920). Written with a refreshing blend of warmth and pungency, its critical acumen springs from true insight and scholarship. Frank Howes's small *Beethoven* (OUP, 'Musical pilgrim' series, 1933) provides a lucid and sensible general introduction, and A E F Dickinson's *Beethoven* (Nelson, 'Discussion books' no 70, 1941) is a penetrating, succinct survey, especially good on the piano music and vocal works. Donald Tovey's *Beethoven* is a posthumous publication, left unfinished at his death. Edited by Hubert Foss (OUP, 1944), it contains a distillation, under various headings, of Tovey's lifelong thought on Beethoven's forms, tonality and musical procedures.

VOCAL MUSIC

Tovey's magnificent series of commentaries on Beethoven's individual works is to be found among the volumes of his *Essays in musical analysis* (OUP, 1935 to 1937). Of these volume V, *Vocal music,* contains a full account of Beethoven's Mass in D and an enlightening programme note for a concert performance of the dungeon scene in *Fidelio;* he uses and commends Edward J Dent's translation of the libretto (OUP, 1938, reprinted 1950, 1957, 1959). The successive overtures to *Fidelio* are dealt with in volume IV, *Illustrative music.*

Berlioz's fine essay on *Fidelio* and its production at the Théâtre Lyrique is embedded in a collection of extracts from *À travers chants* (1862), translated by Edwin Evans senior and misleadingly entitled *A critical study of Beethoven's nine symphonies* (Reeves 1913, reprinted 1958). Richard Northcott's *Beethoven's Fidelio in London* (Press Printers, 1918) is of value to students of operatic history. There is no special study in English on Beethoven's smaller vocal works, but an indispensable guide to his folksong arrangements is provided by Cecil Hopkinson and C B Oldman in their 'Thomson's collections of national song, with special reference to the contributions of Haydn and Beethoven' (Edinburgh Bibliographical Society, *Transactions,* II, 1940).

ORCHESTRAL MUSIC

On the symphonies, concertos and overtures Tovey is again outstanding. Volumes I and II of the *Essays in musical analysis* con-

tain his writings on the symphonies, of which the most important
is the superb extended essay on the Ninth in volume II; the same
volume also contains a remarkable study of the overture *The consecration of the house*. The concertos are dealt with in volume III.
Sir George Grove's *Beethoven and his nine symphonies* (Novello,
1896; *pb* NY, Dover, 1962), based on analytical notes written for
August Manns's Saturday concerts at the Crystal Palace, reflects
the best and most honest in Victorian musical criticism, including
judgments on Beethoven's music made while the composer was
still a living memory. As history it has been superseded by later
scholarship, but its musical insights are still valid.

Berlioz's fiery and imaginative response to Beethoven gives
lasting value to his writings on the symphonies, made available in
English by Edwin Evans senior in the volume of extracts from *A
travers chants* already mentioned. Berlioz is at his best on the
' Pastoral ' and the Ninth. Another composer's reaction, unorthodox
and stimulating, is found in Vaughan Williams's *Some thoughts on
Beethoven's choral symphony with writings on other musical sub-
jects* (OUP, 1953) Edwin Evans's own extremely detailed analyses,
Beethoven's nine symphonies fully described and annotated, were
published in two volumes (Reeves, 1923-24).

For the conductor, Weingartner's study, *On the performance of
Beethoven's symphonies* (Breitkopf and Härtel 1907; *pb* NY,
Dover) is essential reading, springing from a great musician's
thought and practical experience. The adjustments he suggests in
Beethoven's instrumentation are aimed solely at clarifying his intentions, and are based on a scrupulous regard for the distinctive
character of his scoring. The translation by Jessie Crosland is
adequate, but printing and nomenclature have a German cut (*eg
B* for B flat throughout).

STRING QUARTETS

The literature on the string quartets is considerable, and of impressive quality. The most intensive study is *The Beethoven quartets* by
Joseph Kerman (NY, Knopf, 1966; OUP, 1967). He has that intellectual passion which Beethoven himself, according to Bettina Brentano, looked for in a man as the proper response to music. His style

is pungent, and some of his judgments may provoke violent disagreement. But anyone prepared for the effort of following his detailed musical argument with the scores will receive a hundredfold reward in illumination. Another fine study is Daniel Gregory Mason's *The quartets of Beethoven* (NY, OUP, 1947), designed for music lovers prepared to work at the music with miniature scores and records; its value is enhanced by its quotations from D'Indy's various *Cours de composition musicale*, which are not available in English. Joseph de Marliave's frequently quoted *Beethoven's quartets* was a labour of love by a young French musician killed in the 1914-1918 war; a translation by Hilda Andrews, with introduction and notes by Jean Escarra and a preface by Gabriel Fauré, was published in 1928 by OUP (*pb*, Dover, 1961). It makes extensive use of Theodor Helm's *Beethovens Streichquartette* of 1885 (unacknowledged, probably because Marliave did not live to prepare the book for publication). In fact this, and its account of nineteenth century attitudes to the quartets, gives the book some historical interest.

Harold Truscott's *Beethoven's late string quartets* (Denis Dobson, 'The student's music library', edited by Percy M Young, 1968) is concerned to show the continuity between Beethoven's third period and his earlier work, and to act as a guide to the listener prepared to follow both the music and the book itself score in hand. This requires some effort, for the bulk of the 'music examples' are simply references to the score by bar numbers. But it is an effort worth making for anyone who, with Truscott, accepts listening to music as 'a tough business, requiring constant attention'. Philip Radcliffe's *Beethoven's string quartets* (Hutchinson, 'University library', 1965) is an admirable short guide, excellent on the antecedents of Beethoven's quartets, in its use of the sketchbooks, and in its sensitive response to individual works. The quartets are also covered in three booklets in the 'Musical pilgrim' series published by OUP, now unfortunately out of print: *Beethoven's op 18 quartets* by W H Hadow (1926), *Beethoven's second period quartets* by Gerald Abraham (1942) and *Beethoven's last quartets* by Roger Fiske (1940). All three are splendidly written, and combine straightforward analyses (what Abraham calls 'sketch maps') with background information and critical comment. In W W Cobbett's *Cyclopedic survey of chamber music* (OUP, 1929, second edition edited by Colin Mason, 1963) the main Beethoven essay is by Vincent D'Indy and is largely derived from his biography of 1911 mentioned earlier. His analyses are not always convincing, but he is particularly enlightening on Beethoven's variation technique. Cobbett's own additional contribution has his characteristic zestful and practical approach.

VIOLIN SONATAS

On the violin sonatas there are S Midgley's *Handbook to Beethoven's sonatas for violin and pianoforte* (Vincent Music Co, 1911), a simple, enthusiastic descriptive guide for students, and Joseph's Szigeti's *The ten Beethoven sonatas for piano and violin* (Urbana, Illinois, American String Teachers' Association, 1966).

PIANO SONATAS

The literature on the piano sonatas is more extensive. For the serious student Donald Tovey's *A companion to Beethoven's pianoforte sonatas* is indispensable. Published in 1931 by the Associated Board of the Royal Schools of Music, as a commentary on their edition of the sonatas (of which Tovey was joint editor), it contains a detailed analysis of each sonata, interspersed with observations and digressions which Denis Matthews has justly termed ' as witty and revealing as anything in the English language '. It has largely superseded three earlier manuals, though these are sound enough in their way: C Egerton Lowe's *Beethoven's pianoforte sonatas* (Novello, ' Music primers and educational series ', 1921), J Alfred Johnstone's *Notes on the interpretation of twenty four famous piano sonatas by Beethoven* (Reeves, 1927), and Janet A Salisbury's *A concise analysis of Beethoven's pianoforte sonatas* (Weekes, 1931). William Behrend's *Ludwig van Beethoven's pianoforte sonatas* (Dent, 1927), translated, not very happily, by Ingeborg Lund, with an introduction by Alfred Cortot, makes a number of interesting points but is out of date and unduly emotional. Eric Blom's *Beethoven's pianoforte sonatas discussed* (Dent, 1938), based on his annotations for the Beethoven Sonata Society recordings, is

65

aimed at the listener with some musical knowledge. His remark about Beethoven's late fugues ' growing into beauty by an intellectual harnessing of the imagination to a hard task such as is congenial only to creators of the highest type ' is characteristic of the warmth and insight of his approach.

Of the shorter guides, the two volumes entitled *Beethoven: the pianoforte sonatas* by A Forbes Milne in the ' Musical pilgrim ' series (OUP 1925 and 1928) provide helpful analytical notes on a selected dozen sonatas, including the last four. Edwin Fischer's *Beethoven's piano sonatas* (Faber, 1959), translated by Stanley Godman in collaboration with Paul Hamburger, is based on a course of study with his own pupils. His comments, vivid and enlightening as they are, would not mean much without the scores, but his intuitions and practical advice spring from a great pianist's lifelong familiarity with the music. Again, in Denis Matthews's marvellously perceptive *Beethoven piano sonatas* (BBC music guides, 1967) the special insight derived from practical experience as a concert pianist is put to splendid use. The style is admirable, and such technical information as the listener may lack is skilfully given in the context where it is needed.

There remain four specialised studies. Frank Kullak's *Beethoven's piano playing, with an essay on the execution of the trill* (Schirmer, 1901) was written as an introduction to a new critical edition of the piano concertos. Translated by Dr Theodore Baker, it is a careful, scholarly brochure, based on the evidence of Beethoven's friends and pupils such as Czerny, Hummel and Schindler, and could be of real help to any thoughtful executant. So could John B McEwen's *Beethoven: an introduction to an unpublished edition of the pianoforte sonatas* (OUP, 1932), in which a distinguished educator applies his highly personal principles of rhythmic balance to a number of passages from the sonatas, with enlightening effect. John V Cockshoot's *The fugue in Beethoven's piano music* (Routledge & Kegan Paul, ' Studies in the history of music ', 1959) contains detailed analyses of all Beethoven's keyboard fugues and a chapter on the fugal passages embedded in other keyboard works. The analysis is very close, but never loses sensibility and artistic perception. In *Thematic patterns in sonatas of Beethoven* (Faber,

66

1967), Rudolph Reti brings his theory and technique of motivic analysis to bear on a series of works, believing that Beethoven consciously constructed his music out of basic intervals or ' prime cells '. It is a theory that can be a source of light, yet induce scepticism when driven too hard.

MISCELLANEOUS

There is, lastly, a small group of miscellaneous works. Wagner's famous essay on *Beethoven* was conceived as a kind of free oration for the centenary of Beethoven's birth in 1870; a translation by E Dannreuther was published in 1880. Its philosophy springs from that of Schopenhauer, and it must be reckoned with by anyone engaged in the study of musical thought. The issue of *Music and letters* for April 1927, produced in book form to honour the centenary of Beethoven's death, contains some essays of permanent value and interest, notably Edward J Dent's on the Choral Fantasia, and Rebecca Clarke's on ' The quartets as a player sees them '. Paul Mies's *Beethoven's sketches: an analysis of his style based on a study of his sketch books,* translated by Doris L Mackinnon (OUP, 1929; Johnson, NY, 1969) is not easy reading, but provides an absorbing and often moving study of the workings of Beethoven's mind. *Beethoven studies* by Ludwig Misch (University of Oklahoma Press, 1953) is a collection of essays of varying date, length and value, on works as disparate as the *Grosse Fuge* and the ' Battle symphony '. Paul Nettl's *Beethoven encyclopedia* (Peter Owen, 1957) provides a curious miscellany of information, not all of it reliable. *The authentic English editions of Beethoven* by Alan Tyson (Faber, 'All Souls studies' no I, 1963) is an important monograph showing that the English editions of certain major works, including op 106, must be reckoned with among the primary sources for any modern critical edition. Tyson lists individually, with textual notes and variant readings, those works of which authentic editions were published in England.

Editions of Beethoven's music

INTRODUCTION: Any attempt to list the editions of Beethoven's music must start from the fact that from the outset of his career in Vienna his more important works were published, and that most of them bore opus numbers in a regular sequence. This was not so with earlier composers, many of whose works were written for local or occasional use and not published at all. In the case of published works, such opus numbers as they received were usually given by the publisher for his own ease of reference, and often differed from one publisher to another. It was not until much later that it became the normal practice for composers themselves to assign opus numbers to their works, whether published or not. But Beethoven's standing in Vienna put him in an advantageous position in relation to the publishers with whom he dealt, there and elsewhere, who treated the appearance of his first major works as an event, and assigned numbers to them in regular order.

This might be expected to make the task of listing the editions of his works relatively easy. But the position is not so simple as it appears. The opus numbers relate entirely to the order of publication and cannot be relied on in determining the order of composition, especially where Beethoven resuscitated early works in order to raise money. Many smaller works, moreover, both early and late, especially those discovered or published after his death, never received opus numbers at all.

THEMATIC CATALOGUES
The earliest thematic catalogue of Beethoven's works actually appeared during his lifetime, in 1819. It was produced by the

Leipzig publisher Friedrich Hofmeister, and was intended to be the first of a series devoted to the instrumental music of 'the most famous composers of our time'; it was confined to works with opus numbers. The first to make any claim to completeness was the catalogue published in 1851 by the Leipzig firm of Breitkopf & Härtel; the compiler's name was not stated. This aimed to include all Beethoven's published works, and the list of those with opus numbers was followed by a list of those without, classified by instruments. In 1868 Breitkopf & Härtel, who had in the meantime begun to bring out a complete edition of Beethoven's works, published a new thematic catalogue by the great Beethoven scholar Gustav Nottebohm. This was a bigger affair altogether, and included all Beethoven's works currently available from German music dealers, with dates of composition and first performance. Once more, the works with opus numbers were listed first; then followed a classified list of works without an opus number, a short list of doubtful and spurious works and a bibliography. This remained for many years the standard catalogue, and was reprinted many times; the reprint of 1913 contained a chronological survey, compiled by Emerich Kastner, of all the books and articles about Beethoven that had appeared from the year of his death. A further reprint, with supplementary material by Theodor Frimmel, appeared in 1925 (Breitkopf).

It was in the late 1930's that the great scholar Georg Kinsky, of Cologne, conceived the idea of expanding his study of the early editions of Beethoven's works so as to embody the results of his own and other more recent researches in a fully comprehensive catalogue which should supersede that of Nottebohm and do for Beethoven what Köchel's catalogue had done for Mozart. The 1939-45 war uprooted him from Cologne, and in the course of it he lost not only his home but most of his scholarly material. He had, however, been persuaded by the music librarian of the Bavarian State Library, Dr Hans Halm, with whom he had been in correspondence over his project, to send a copy of the typescript to Munich for greater safety. Although Munich later suffered as severely as Cologne from air attack, the typescript survived, and after the war Halm urged him to carry on and complete his work, which the newly founded publishing house of Henle declared itself willing to publish. He was at length prevailed upon to take up the task once more, but died in 1951, at the age of sixty nine, with his work still unfinished. Halm then undertook the delicate and difficult task of revising and completing Kinsky's work, and the catalogue appeared at last in 1955 under Kinsky's name, 'completed and edited' by Halm. (The full title runs: *Das Werk Beethovens: thematisch-bibliographisches Verzeichnis seiner sämtlichen vollendeten Kompositionen von Georg Kinsky. Nach dem Tode des Verfassers abgeschlossen und herausgegeben von Hans Halm.*)

'Kinsky-Halm' thus took its place as a fully comprehensive and scholarly catalogue of all Beethoven's finished works (those completed by him, or left unfinished and completed by others, but excluding those merely sketched). The basic distinction between works with and without opus number is maintained, and the section devoted to works without opus number now provides a standard framework of reference and numbering. In the catalogue itself the numbers in this section are prefixed by the abbreviation 'WoO' (Werk ohne Opuszahl), but for general use it seems preferable to adopt the initials KH: thus the variations for piano and cello on 'See the conquering hero comes' would be cited as KH45.

COMPLETE EDITIONS

The idea of producing a complete edition (CE) of Beethoven's works was raised more than once during his lifetime, but came to nothing. The first complete edition was begun by Breitkopf & Härtel in 1862, under the title *Beethovens Werke. Vollständige kritisch überall berechtigte Ausgabe.* It was arranged in twenty four series; a supplementary volume completed the edition in 1880:

    I Symphonies
    II Other orchestral works (excluding overtures)
    III Overtures
    IV Works for violin and orchestra
    V Chamber works for five instruments and over
    VI String quartets
    VII String trios
    VIII Works for wind instruments

IX Works for piano and orchestra
X Piano quintet and quartets
XI Piano trios
XII Works for piano and violin
XIII Works for piano and cello
XIV Works for piano and wind instruments
XV Piano duets
XVI Piano sonatas
XVII Variations for piano
XVIII Smaller piano pieces
XIX Church music
XX Works for the stage
XXI Cantatas
XXII Vocal works with orchestra
XXIII Vocal works with piano
XXIV Songs with piano, violin and cello (*ie* the folk song arrangements)
XXV Supplement.

The editors were not named, but the original sources were used, and the edition as a whole was reasonably authoritative as far as it went. A number of works were issued singly, *eg* the symphonies. The Breitkopf edition is reprinted complete by Edwin F Kalmus (PO Box 47, Huntington Station, LI, NY 11746), and by Universal Edition, London. Sonatas and other works for piano solo and most of the chamber works are reprinted in Lea Pocket Scores.

Later research made it apparent, however, that in certain groups the Breitkopf edition was incomplete, and in 1957 Willy Hess brought out his catalogue of the 335 authentic (and 66 doubtful or spurious) works not included in the CE. In 1959 he began to produce for Breitkopf & Härtel (now in Wiesbaden) a series of supplementary volumes. The following have appeared so far:

I Unaccompanied Italian part songs
II Vocal works with orchestra
III Works for solo instruments and orchestra
IV Orchestral works
V Songs with piano accompaniment, canons and musical jokes
VI Chamber music for strings

VII Chamber music including wind instruments, and works for musical clock
VIII Piano arrangements of his own works
IX Piano works and chamber music including piano
X and XI *Leonora*, the original version of 1805
XII Dramatic works, vol 2
XIII Folk song arrangements
XIV Folk song arrangements.

Meanwhile, in 1961, the firm of Henle in Munich, which had brought out 'Kinsky-Halm', began the publication of a new complete edition under the direction of Joseph Schmidt-Görg, director of the Beethoven-Archiv in Bonn. This is proceeding extremely slowly; the only series in which any volumes have appeared so far are the following: series III, works for solo instruments with orchestra, series IV, chamber music with piano, series VI, chamber music for strings, and series VII, piano music. It is thus apparent that for the bulk of Beethoven's works the Breitkopf CE, with Willy Hess's supplementary volumes, remains the standard edition.

SKETCH BOOKS

A word must be said about the published editions of Beethoven's sketch books, although their use demands a knowledge of German (and in one case of Russian), because they are a unique manifestation of his creative processes. They were first studied in detail by Nottebohm, who described and discussed a number of them in various essays later published in successive volumes of his *Beethoveniana*. In 1865 and 1880 he published extended extracts and descriptions of two of them, including the one containing the 'Great Sketch' for the first movement of the 'Eroica' symphony. These were reissued by Breitkopf in 1924 under the title *Zwei Skizzenbücher von Beethoven aus den Jahren 1801 bis 1803*, with a foreword by Paul Mies, whose book on the sketchbooks had just appeared (the translation is referred to on p 67). In 1924 the Beethovenhaus in Bonn produced a facsimile of one of the sketchbooks, transcribed by Arnold Schmitz; then, in 1952, the Beethovenhaus began what is intended to be a complete critical edition of the sketchbooks. Three volumes have so far appeared, edited by

Joseph Schmidt-Görg and Dagmar Weise and covering, among other works, the Mass in D, the Choral Fantasy, the 'Pastoral' symphony and the op 70 piano trios.

Other published sketch books are the one edited by K H Mikulicz and published by Breitkopf in 1927, and those in Russian, dating from 1802 and 1803 and containing material for the 'Eroica' symphony and the 'Kreutzer' sonata, of which facsimiles, edited and transcribed by N L Fishman, were published by the State Music Publishers in Moscow in 1962. The so-called 'Kafka Sketchbook' (BM Add MS 29801 ff 39-162) is due for publication in facsimile in 1970 (BM and Royal Musical Association), with transcription and commentary by Joseph Kerman.

OTHER EDITIONS

All editions are in score unless otherwise stated, and the word ' by ' is here equivalent to ' edited by ' or ' arranged by '. Publishers' names are given in full except for the following:

OUP = Oxford University Press
UE = Universal Edition (Vienna or London)
WPV = Wiener Philharmonischer Verlag (Vienna)
Br = Breitkopf & Härtel (Leipzig or Wiesbaden)
Eul = Eulenburg
s/c = Schirmer/Chappell (New York, London).

Where no town is given, the place of publication is London. The place of publication and the editor's first name are omitted when either recurs several times in succession. Publishers' addresses are most readily available in the *British catalogue of music* (issued by the British National Bibliography), which is to be found in major public libraries throughout the world. Besides the addresses of all British music publishers, this catalogue includes those of the leading American firms and those of many European firms which have branches or agencies in London.

The lists that follow do not aim to provide an exhaustive catalogue of the many editions, selections and arrangements in which Beethoven's works appear; such a task is clearly impossible within the scope of a short book. Their purpose is rather to meet the everyday needs of performance and study while keeping in mind those standards of editing which modern musical research has led us to expect. The general principle of selection may be outlined as follows: scholarly quality and the consequent value of the text or editorial preface, or of both; the historical interest of the editor or arranger as a famous performer or teacher; the fact that an edition may represent the only form in which the work in question is at present available; the interest of an arrangement, in an unusual but convenient medium. In addition to well-edited pocket or miniature scores, some useful ones without editor's name have also been included.

Vocal music

Masses: The beautiful, neglected Mass in C, op 86, and the Mass in D, op 123, with its unique and profoundly personal sublimities (though the title 'missa solemnis' usually given to it originally meant no more than that all parts of the liturgical text were set to music): in score, with copious textual notes, both by Willy Hess (Eul), no editor (wpv); vocal scores: Mass in C, by Berthold Tours, with Latin text and English translation by the Rev J Troutbeck (Novello); Mass in D, by Kurt Soldan (Peters), no editor (Novello, s/c). The autograph of the Kyrie of the Mass in D, in facsimile, by Wilhelm Virneisel (Schneider, Tutzing).

Oratorio: The very uneven *Christus am Oelberge* ('The Mount of Olives'), vocal score, with German text, by Carl Reinecke (Br) and Alfred Dörffel (Peters), and with the Rev J Troutbeck's translation, by Ebenezer Prout (Novello); a version to an adapted text, in German and English, under the title *Engedi, or David in the wilderness* (Novello). The final chorus 'Welte singen' (Hallelujah) with its spacious fugue, by Walter Ehret (Boosey), by C F Manney (B F Wood Music Co, Boston), arranged for four part men's chorus by Fenno Heath, and for school chorus by R L Baldwin (both s/c).

Other choral works: The early cantata on the death of the Emperor Joseph II, KH87, with its hints of greater things to come, vocal score, with English translation, by Elliot Forbes (s/c; also with a Latin translation by C J McNaspy). The Choral Fantasy, op 80, for piano, chorus and orchestra, a curious trial run of ideas and procedures later fulfilled in the ninth symphony, in score, by

Willy Hess (Eul), and the choral final section in vocal score, with English translation, by Robert Elkin (Novello). *Meeresstille und glückliche Fahrt,* op 112, a short, impressive setting for chorus and orchestra of two poems by Goethe, vocal score, by Carl Reinecke (Br) and with the Rev J Troutbeck's translation, no editor (Novello). *Der glorreiche Augenblick* (' The glorious moment '), op 136, an occasional cantata written at the time of the Congress of Vienna, vocal score with German and English text, by Hermann Scherchen (Ars Viva, Mainz).

Operas: *Fidelio,* the final version in two acts by G F Treitschke (the one now everywhere accepted and performed), in score, by W Altmann (Eul); vocal score, by Artur Bodnansky, translated by Theodore Baker (s/c), by Ernest Roth, translated by Edward J Dent (Boosey) and by Kurt Soldan, German text (Peters). The first version of 1805, lovingly reconstructed by Erich Prieger, was published in 1905 as a centenary tribute, in vocal score, under its original title *Leonore* (Br). Prieger also produced for private circulation a very few copies of the full score. It is this publication, photographically reproduced and carefully edited, annotated and corrected by Willy Hess, which forms volumes X and XI of the supplementary volumes to the CE. For the four overtures which Beethoven wrote at successive stages see p 81. *Vestas Feuer* (' The vestal flame '), begun in 1803 but abandoned after only a few numbers were completed: a scene for vocal quartet and orchestra has been edited from the autograph and completed by Willy Hess (full score, Brucknerverlag, Wiesbaden; vocal score, Alkor, Kassel).

Works for solo voice and orchestra: The big soprano scena *Ah, perfido,* op 65, by Max Unger (Eul); the scena and aria *No, non turbati,* KH92a, for soprano and string orchestra, in score with piano reduction, by Willy Hess (Brucknerverlag, Wiesbaden); the duet for soprano and tenor *Nei giorni tuoi felici,* KH93, full, miniature and piano scores by Willy Hess (Eul). The last two published for the first time.

Part songs and canons: The melodious unaccompanied Italian partsongs written by the young Beethoven as exercises for Salieri are contained in volume I of the CE supplementary volumes edited by Willy Hess. The *Elegische Gesang,* op 118, a touching memorial to the wife of a friend, Baron Pasqualati, originally for SATB and string quartet, arranged with organ accompaniment by Herbert Zipper (Augener). The popular Chorus of Dervishes from the incidental music to *The ruins of Athens* (Boosey). The arietta *In questa tomba oscura*, KH133, arranged for male voice chorus by Y Davidoff, translation by M Kernochan (Galaxy Music Corporation, NY). There are many partsong arrangements of ' Die Ehre Gottes aus der Natur ', the most famous of the settings of six religious poems by Gellert, op 48 (the title is sometimes translated as ' Creation's Hymn '); the third of the set, ' Vom Tode ' (of death) has been arranged for four part unaccompanied chorus with English text by W J Wager (S/C). Selections from the rounds and canons, many of them originating in private jokes and social occasions, in *Acht Singkanons*, by Willy Hess (Hug, Zurich); *Rounds and canons by Beethoven*, by W G Whittaker, English texts by A G Latham (OUP).

Solo songs with piano: Complete, no editor (Peters). Selections : *Lieder*, no editor (Schott) containing all six Gellert songs, *An die ferne Geliebte*, and a few others; Six songs for high voice/low voice, by H E Krehbiel, translated by Theodore Baker (S/C). The lovely song cycle *An die ferne Geliebte* (' To the distant beloved '), in which the songs are linked by the continuous flow of the accompaniment, by the great accompanist Gerald Moore, translated by Marjorie Wardle and Fabian Smith (Elkin), by H E Krehbiel, translated by Theodore Baker (S/C), and by Max Friedländer (Insel Verlag, Liepzig). Single songs : *Adelaïde,* op 46, translated by Steuart Wilson, and *An die Hoffnung* (' To hope '), op 94, Beethoven's second setting of Tiedge's poem, translated by A H Fox Strangways (both OUP); ' Wonne der Wehmuth ' and ' Sehnsucht ', from the three Goethe settings of op 83, translated as ' Tears of love ' and ' Longing ', and ' Die Ehre Gottes aus der Natur ' and ' Gottes Macht und Vorsehung ', translated as ' Nature's praise of God ' and ' The power of God ', all translations by H Stevens (Augener). A curiosity is the facsimile of the autograph of the little song *Zärtliche Liebe* (' Ich liebe dich, so wie du mich '); the MS belonged at one time to Schubert, who inadvertently noted down part of a sonata movement on a blank side, and later gave one of the pages to his friend Anselm Hüttenbrenner. Brahms subsequently acquired both pages and made a note of the date on the MS. The facsimile bears the title *The autograph of three masters, Beethoven, Schubert, Brahms* ('Harrow replicas' no 1, Heffer, Cambridge). The song has also been edited by Carl Deis (S/C).

Folk song arrangements: Beethoven was for many years in contact with the Edinburgh music publisher George Thomson, for whose successive collections of Scottish, Welsh and Irish airs Haydn had produced over four hundred arrangements for voice and piano with violin and cello. Beethoven's are fewer in number but more varied; some are for duet or vocal trio and one or two even include passages for choir. Like Haydn's, they show no awareness of the idiom of these folk melodies and its harmonic implications, but many of them are full of character and real power. There are various selections in modern editions:—Irish airs: *Three Irish folk songs*, arranged for two part chorus of women's voices with piano accompaniment by Elliott Forbes (S/C), 'Soldier's song' (the tune is that sung to Thomas Moore's 'The harp that once through Tara's halls'), arranged for four part male chorus with piano accompaniment by Robert Hernried (S/C). Two Irish songs and a Welsh song ('O would that I were that sweet linnet', 'He promised me at parting' and 'The dream') have been arranged for solo voice from their duet originals by Gerald Moore (OUP). Scottish airs: the Scottish song arrangements published as op 108, with the title *25 Schottische Lieder*, by L Benda (Litolff); 'Faithfu' Johnnie' and 'Charlie is my darling', arranged for three part women's chorus and piano by Robert Hernried (S/C). Finally a group of folksongs from many countries, KH158, for solo voice with accompaniment for piano, violin and cello, originally prepared for Thomson but never published, was edited from the autographs by Georg Schünemann with the title *Neues Volksliederheft*, piano score and string parts (Br).

Orchestral music

Symphonies: Complete series, in score: no 1 in C op 21, no 2 in D op 36, no 3 in E flat (the 'Eroica') op 55, no 4 in B flat op 60, no 5 in C minor op 67, no 6 in F (the 'Pastoral') op 68, no 7 in A op 92, no 8 in F op 93, no 9 in D minor (the 'Choral') op 125. By Max Unger (Eul); by Marc Pincherle and Maurice Bellecour (Heugel, Paris); no editor (Hawkes, Kalmus of NY, Ricordi, WPV); by Anis Fuleihan, study and conducting format with piano arrangement (Southern Music Publishing Co, NY); by A E Wier (Heffer, Cambridge, Miniature Arrow score series). This last is printed with four miniature score 'pages' to one large page, with principal themes indicated by a system of arrows and underlinings designed to help the beginner at score reading.

Smaller groups, in score: no 1-3, 5, 7, 9, by Gordon Jacob (Penguin).

Piano arrangements, complete series: By Franz Liszt (Br); by Ernst Pauer (Augener, S/C). Piano duet: by Hugo Ulrich (Peters), by Alfredo Casella (Ricordi), no transcriber named (S/C). Liszt's arrangement is a great composer's attempt to use the resources of the nineteenth century piano to capture the finer nuances of Beethoven's scoring. It demands an advanced technique and a hand capable of stretching tenths.

Single works: No 5, facsimile of the autograph, by Georg Schünemann (Maximilian Verlag, Berlin); no 6, as piano duet by Daniel Gregory Mason (Schirmer); no 9, facsimile of the autograph (Kistner & Siegel, Leipzig); vocal score, with piano arrangement of the entire symphony by Berthold Tours (Novello).

Concertos and concerto movements

Piano: Complete series, in score: no 1 in C op 15, no 2 in B flat op 19, no 3 in C minor op 37, no 4 in G op 58, no 5 in E flat (the 'Emperor') op 73. By Wilhelm Altmann, with Beethoven's cadenzas to no 1-4 (Eul); by A E Wier (Longman's Miniature Arrow score series vol 8, NY); no editor (Hawkes).

Smaller groups and single works: No 3-5, no editor (Ricordi); no 4, no editor (WPV). The little concerto in E flat, KH4 (1784), of which all that has survived is a MS copy of the piano part with corrections by Beethoven, has been reconstructed by Willy Hess (Musikwissenschaftlicher Verlag, Leipzig, and Eul). The Rondo in B flat for piano and orchestra, KH6, dating from about 1795, may possibly have been the original finale for the B flat piano concerto op 19; it has been published with the orchestral accompaniment arranged for string quartet by Alexander Feinland and Watson Forbes (score and parts, Hinrichsen).

Arrangements for two pianos: no 1 to 5, by T F Dunhill, with compressed score of the accompaniment for second piano by Adam Carse (Augener); by Franz Kullak, introduction and notes translated by Theodore Baker (S/C); no 5 by Max Pauer (Peters).

Cadenzas: Busoni's edition of Beethoven's own cadenzas to no 1, 3 and 4, first published in 1901, was reissued in 1950 (Heinrichshofen, Wilhelmshaven). There are also cadenzas to the same concertos by Edwin Fischer, keeping strictly within the Beethoven idiom (Schott), and to the first four concertos by Ignaz Friedman, demanding virtuosity but not too turgid (S/C). Clara Schumann's cadenzas to no 3 and 4 have been published by Peters. Both Gabriel Fauré's sensitive cadenzas to no 3 (Pierre Schneider, Paris) and Erno von Dohnányi's to no 4 (Arcadia Music Publishing Co), provide a close and thoughtful commentary by one creative mind on another, while Donald Tovey's cadenzas to no 4 are introduced by a characteristically illuminating foreword (OUP). A remarkable Russian publication is the collection of seventeen cadenzas to no 4 edited by K S Sorokin (State Music Publishing, Moscow); it includes names of great historic interest, among them Beethoven's pupil Moscheles, Brahms, von Bülow, Rubinstein, Medtner, d'Albert, Saint-Saëns and Busoni.

Violin: C major, incomplete, KH5. Of this early work, dating from Beethoven's last years in Bonn, only part of the first movement has survived. It was first published in 1875, edited and completed by Joseph Hellmesberger, who added trumpets and drums to the score and treated it in a somewhat inflated style. A more recent edition, under the title *Konzertstück für Violine und Orchester*, by Juan Manen (UE) retains Beethoven's original scoring: in completing the piece the editor has scrupulously refrained from introducing harmonic elements alien to Beethoven's early style.

D major, op 61. In score, by Alan Tyson (Eul), an admirable and definitive edition; by A E Wier (Longman's Miniature Arrow Score series, vol 7, NY); no editor (Hawkes, WPV, Ricordi). With piano accompaniment, by Josef Szigeti, with score of three cadenzas by

Busoni and parts for strings and tympani to accompany the first (Curci, Milan); of this edition the violinist Neville Marriner wrote (*Musical times* November 1963 p 809): 'Just to read the preface and the notes is equivalent to a Master Class given by Szigeti himself. To play through the score adopting the printed recommendations for phrasing and fingering is to experience a revelation of style and musicianship from a man who literally and figuratively stands head and shoulders above violinists today.' Other editions by Leopold Auer (Fischer, NY), by Carl Flesch, with cadenzas (Peters), by Émile Sauret (Augener) and by Henry Schradieck, with cadenzas (s/c).

Cadenzas: The cadenzas which Beethoven wrote for the piano transcription of the concerto which he dedicated to Stefan von Breuning's wife had been transcribed for violin by Max Rostal (Hawkes 1938, Novello 1949) and by Wolfgang Schneiderhan, whose edition also contains the original piano version (Henle, Munich). Other cadenzas are by Fritz Kreisler (Schott), Donald Tovey (OUP), Ferruccio Bonavia (Novello, in *Short cadenzas for the Beethoven and Brahms Violin Concertos*) and Tossy Spiwakowsky (Br).

Triple concerto, op 56, for piano, violin and cello. In score, by W Altmann (Eul), by A E Wier (Longman's Miniature Arrow Score series, vol 7, NY), no editor (Hawkes). Arranged for violin, cello and two pianos by J Guschenskaya, violin and cello parts edited by David Oistrakh and Sviatoslav Knuschewizky (State Music Publishing, Moscow); for two pianos by Hugo Ulrich (Peters).

Romances for violin and orchestra: No 1 in G op 40 and no 2 in F op 50. In score, no editor (Eul). Arranged for violin and piano, by Leopold Auer (Fischer, NY), by Max Rostal (Novello), by Henry Schradieck (s/c); singly, for violin and piano, by Maxim Jacobsen (Peters) and no 2, for flute and piano, by Joseph Slater (Rudall Carte).

The little *Romance cantabile* in E minor, not included in KH and possibly the middle movement of a lost early work, for piano, flute and bassoon accompanied by strings and two oboes, has been completed and edited by Willy Hess (Br).

Overtures, incidental and ballet music

Overtures: ie *Prometheus* (Ballet), *Coriolan, Leonora* no 1, 2 and 3, *Fidelio, Egmont, Ruins of Athens,* C major op 115 (*Name day*), King Stephen, C major op 124 (*The consecration of the house*). Complete series, in score, by Max Unger (Eul), by Anis Fuleihan, study and conducting format with piano arrangement (Southern Publishing Co, NY), no editor (WPV).

Smaller groups and single works, in score: Prometheus, Coriolan, Egmont, Leonora no 3, *Fidelio,* no editor (Hawkes); *Coriolan, Egmont, Leonora* no 3, no editor (Ricordi); *Coriolan* and *Egmont* (one volume), by Gordon Jacob (Penguin).

Arrangements: For piano conductor and orchestral parts, by A Winter, *Leonora* no 3 and *Ruins of Athens* (Hawkes); for piano, solo and duet, all overtures, by Richard Kleinmichel (Peters).

Incidental and ballet music: In score: *Egmont,* incidental music, no editor (Eul); *Tarpeja,* Introduction to act II and Triumphal March, KH-2a and 2b, by Georg Schünemann (Schott).

Arrangements: Prometheus, two dances, piano conductor and orchestral parts, by Harold Perry (Hawkes); *Egmont,* March, conductor's condensed score and band parts, by Roger Smith (Mercury Music Corporation, NY).

Piano arrangements: Beethoven's own piano arrangement of the *Ritterballet,* KH1, is in volume VIII of Willy Hess's supplementary volumes to the CE (Br); also by Ernst Pauer (Augener); *Prometheus,* complete ballet music, by Richard Metzdorff (Litolff, Brunswick); *Ruins of Athens,* Turkish March, by A Rubinstein (Boosey).

Smaller pieces

Three Equali for four trombones, KH30. Score and parts (Briegel, NY); for no 1 arranged for military band instruments see under March, KH29.

Dances in score: Six *Gesellschafts-Menuette* for two violins and cello, KH9, score and parts, by Georg Kinsky, piano accompaniment ad lib by F Willms (Schott); in Kinsky's opinion it is not certain whether this, and other sets of dances scored for string trio, represent the original version or an arrangement of a set originally scored for orchestra. Twelve Minuets for Orchestra (*Zwölf Menuette für Orchester* KH12), by Willy Hess (Nagel, Kassel). Twelve Contretänze (*Zwölf Contretänze für Orchester* KH14), by Walter Kolneder (Schott); Eleven Viennese Dances (*Elf Wiener Tänze, ie* the ' Mödling ' dances, KH17), by Hugo Riemann (Br).

Dances—arrangements: Gratulations-Menuett, KH3, for piano solo and piano duet by Felix Guenther (Century Music Publishing Co, NY). Six Minuets for orchestra, KH10, no 3, 5, 2, for double bass and piano, as *Drei Menuettos für Kontrabass und Klavier,* by H Samuel Sterling (Peters, Hinrichsen). Twelve Contretänze, KH14, for viola and piano, as Country Dance, by Watson Forbes and Alan Richardson (OUP). A selection of dances from various groups, for piano duet, as *Tänze für Orchester,* by Theodor Kirchner (Peters).

Marches: Marsch für Militärmusik, KH24. Score and parts, adapted by Felix Greissle (S/C). March for 2 clarinets, 2 horns and 2 bassoons, KH29, for 2 B flat cornets or trumpets, horn, trombone, baritone and tuba by G W Lotzenhiser (Rubank, Chicago; with ' Chorale ', *ie* no 1 of Three Equali for four trombones, KH30).

Chamber music

Octet in E flat, op 103, for 2 oboes, 2 clarinets, 2 horns, 2 bassoons, an early work despite its opus number, written in Bonn for the Elector Max Franz's small wind band, by W Altmann (Eul); its sparkling one-in-a-bar minuet, as ' Scherzo ', for 3 B flat clarinets, E flat alto or fourth B flat, and B flat bass clarinet, by Clair W Johnson (Rubank, Chicago). For Beethoven's revised version of this work see the string quintet op 4. Rondino in E flat, KH25, another Bonn work for wind octet as above, no editor (Eul, Ricordi).

Septet, op 20, for clarinet, horn, bassoon, violin, viola, cello and double bass, by W Altmann (Eul), no editor (Hawkes, Ricordi); for piano duet by Hugo Ulrich (Peters), and for 2 pianos, 4 players by Ernst Pauer (Augener). Composed in the same year as the first symphony, the septet became so popular and successful that Beethoven could hardly bear to hear it mentioned.

Sextets: op 71, for 2 clarinets, 2 horns, 2 bassoons, and op 81 b, for string quartet and 2 horns, no editor (Eul); for piano duet by Hugo Ulrich and Robert Wittmann, with op 16, as *Klavierquintett und Sextette op 16, 71 und 81b* (Peters); op 81b for 2 horns and piano by Bernhard Krol (Simrock, Hamburg).

String quintets: in E flat op 4 (Beethoven's recast and improved version of the wind octet op 103), in C minor op 104 (the composer's arrangement of the piano trio op 1 no 3), in C major op 29, a fine work overshadowed by the string quartets, Fugue in D, op 137, composed in 1817 but published posthumously, all no editor (Eul). Quintet in E flat op 16 for piano, oboe, clarinet, bassoon and horn, score, no editor (Eul), score and parts no editor (Musica Rara); Beethoven's own arrangement for piano, violin, viola and cello, score, no editor (Eul), score and parts, no editor (s/c); for piano duet, see above under Sextets. Quintet for oboe, 3 horns and bassoon, an incomplete autograph, not in KH, completed by L A Zellner in 1862, score and parts, by Willy Hess (Schott).

String quartets: Complete series, in score, by W Altmann (Eul), no editor (Hawkes, Ricordi, WPV); in the recent WPV edition of op 130 the Grosse Fuge is given as finale, with the second finale of 1826 as an appendix. In parts, by Engelbert Röntgen (Br), by Joseph Joachim and Andreas Moser (Peters), by H Withers (Augener), no editor (s/c). Op 18 no 1 to 6, in score, by Paul Mies (Bärenreiter); parts, by F Hermann (Augener), by Andreas Moser and Kurt Soldan (Peters), by Paul Mies (Henle). The first version of op 18 no 1, by Joseph Wedig (Beethovenhaus, Bonn), by Paul Mies (Bärenreiter). Beethoven's version for string quartet of the piano sonata op 14 no 1, no editor (Eul). Preludes and Fugues for string quartet in F and C, by Willy Hess (Nagel, Kassel); these are early works, not listed in KH but published by Willy Hess in volume VI of his Supplement to the CE. For Beethoven's own arrangement of the Grosse Fuge, op 133, for piano duet, see below p 86.

For violin, viola and cello. Trios—without piano: Op. 3 in E flat, no editor (Eul); arranged as a piano sonata, possibly by Beethoven himself, by Eugene Hartzell (Doblinger, Vienna). Serenade, op 8, no editor (Eul); parts, by Carl Herrmann and Paul Grummer (Peters); version for viola and piano, as Notturno op 42, see p 85. Op 9 no 1 in G, 2 in D, 3 in C minor (a fine set, of which no 3 in C minor opens with a theme foreshadowing one of the pervading motifs in the late quartets), by W Altmann (Eul).

Serenade in D, op 25, for flute, violin and viola, a delightful work, written with sensitive imagination, score, no editor (Eul, Ricordi); parts, by Carl Herrmann (Peters). Walter Bergmann has chosen and arranged a series of movements from op 8 and op 25 to form a Serenade for three recorders (Schott: two descant and treble).

Trio in C, op 87, for 2 oboes and cor anglais, score, no editor (Eul, Hawkes); score and parts, no editor (Boosey); arranged for descant, treble and tenor recorders by Edgar Hunt (Schott); for three violas, by Lionel Tertis (Bosworth), menuetto and finale for three B flat clarinets, by H Voxman, score and parts (Rubank, Chicago).

Variations on 'Là ci darem', KH28, for 2 oboes and cor anglais, by Fritz Stein, score and parts (Br); for clarinet and piano by Simeon Bellison (Fischer, NY) and for flute, oboe, clarinet, bassoon and horn by Simeon Bellison (Ricordi).

Trios—for piano, violin and cello: Op 1 no 1 in E flat, 2 in G, 3 in C minor; op 11 in B flat (for piano, clarinet or violin and cello); op 70 no 1 in D, 2 in E flat; op 97 in B flat (the 'Archduke'); Variations on a theme of Wenzel Müller (' Ich bin der Schneider Kakadu ') op 121a. Complete series, score and parts, by Günter Raphael (Henle), the most recent and reliable edition; no editor, and excluding the variations op 121a but including the small trios KH38 and 39 (Augener); by Joseph Adamowski (s/c, separate numbers). In score, op 1 no 1 to 3 by Max Unger, op 11, no editor, op 70 no 1 and 2, no editor, op 97 by Wilhelm Altmann, Variations op 121a (all Eul). Of the early Variations on an original theme, op 44, ten have been arranged for piano solo by Joseph Müller-Blattau (see below p 88).

Duos—violin and piano: Sonatas, Op 12 no 1 in D, 2 in A, 3 in E flat; op 23 in A minor; op 24 in F (the ' Spring '); op 30 no 1 in A, no 2 in C minor, no 3 in G; op 47 in A (the ' Kreutzer '); op 96 in G. Complete series, by Joseph Joachim (Peters), by Max Jacobsen (Peters), by Ruth Ganz and Leopold Auer (Fischer, NY), by Adolph Brodsky and Max Vogrich (s/c), by Walther Lampe and Kurt Schäffer (Henle). Single works. Op 24, score for violin and piano, with viola part, by Watson Forbes (Peters); its syncopated scherzo, for four B flat clarinets and bassoon, by George Draper (OUP). Rondo in G, KH41, for viola and piano by Watson Forbes (Schott),

for horn and piano by Lorenzo Sansone and Pietro Ballatore (s/c).
Eleven variations on 'Se vuol ballare', KH40, for piano solo by
Joseph Müller-Blattau, see below p 88.

Duos—Viola and piano: Notturno, op 42, an arrangement of the
Serenade for string trio, op 8, probably made by F X Kleinheinz but
revised by Beethoven; by William Primrose (Schott), by Sydney
Beck (s/c). The fifth movement as *Alla polacca* by Watson
Forbes (OUP). Beck's edition makes considerable changes in the
original arrangement to make it more rewarding for the viola,
giving it some of the material from the piano part.

Cello and piano: Sonatas, Op 5 no 1 in F, no 2 in G minor; op
69 in A; op 102 no 1 in C, no 2 in D. Complete series by Donald
Tovey and Percy Such (Augener), by Leo Schulz (s/c), by Carl
Reinecke (Br). Op 5 no 2 arranged for viola by Lionel Tertis, edited
by Donald Tovey (Augener).

Variations: 'See the conquering hero comes', KH45, 'Ein
Mädchen oder Weibchen', op 66 and 'Bei Männern, welche Liebe
fühlen', KH46, by Hans Münch-Holland and Günther Henle
(Henle), by Carl Reinecke (Br), by Joachim Stutschewsky (Peters),
by Percy Such (Augener).

Arrangements: op 66 for viola by Lionel Tertis (variations 1-8,
10, 12, Hawkes). KH45, for cello and orchestra by Anthony Collins
(Bosworth), for tuba and piano by W J Bell (Fischer, NY). KH46
for viola and piano by Watson Forbes (Hinrichsen), for double
bass and piano by Hans Fryba (Weinberger, Vienna), for two
pianos by Pierre Luboschutz (Fischer, NY).

Mandoline and piano: Beethoven probably wrote these little
pieces in Vienna about 1795-6 for his friend and admirer Wenzel
Krumpholz. Sonatinas in C minor, KH43 no 1 and C major KH44
no 1, Adagio in E flat KH43 no 2 and Air and Variations in D
KH44 no 2, by V Hladky, founder of the Wiener Mandolinen-
Kammermusik-Vereinigung (Musikverlag V Hladky, Vienna).
Arrangements: KH43 no 1 for violin and piano by T F Dunhill
(Williams), for cello and piano by J Stutschewsky and I Thaler
(Hinrichsen); KH44 no 1 for piano solo by Felix van Dyck (s/c).
KH43 no 2 and 44 no 2 for viola and piano by K M Komma
(Ichthys Verlag, Stuttgart).

Viola and cello: Duet in E flat, KH32, which Beethoven called ' Duett für zwei obligaten Augengläser (Duet for two obligato eyeglasses), probably a joke at the expense of the shortsighted Baron Zmeskall. First movement as ' Sonata movement ' by Fritz Stein, Minuet by Karl Haas (both Peters/Hinrichsen).

Horn and Piano: Sonata op 17, by Max Wolff (Hawkes), by Edmond Leloir (Simrock, Hamburg and London); for cello and piano by Percy Such (Augener).

Clarinet and Bassoon: Three duos, KH27; for violin and cello by Friedrich Hermann (Peters), for piano, violin and cello by A Mann (Augener).

Piano music

Piano duet: The small group of works which Beethoven composed for piano duet has recently been edited by Karl Heinz Füssl, under the title *Werke fur Klavier zu vier Händen* (UE); the volume contains the sonata in D op 6, three marches op 45, the variations composed in Bonn on a theme by Count Waldstein, KH67, and those on a melody to Goethe's poem ' Ich denke dein ', KH74, written in 1800 for Therese Brunsvik and her sister Josephine Deym. Beethoven also arranged the Grosse Fuge, op 133, for piano duet. Published after his death as op 134, his arrangement appears in volume VIII of Willy Hess's supplement to the CE, it has also been edited and transcribed for two pianos by Harold Bauer (s/c).

Piano Solo: Sonatas, complete series. By Donald Tovey and Harold Craxton (Associated Board of the Royal Schools of Music), by Stewart Macpherson (J Williams), by Frederick Lamond (Br), by Franz Liszt, revised by Edward Watson (Bosworth), by Béla Bartók and Erno von Dohnányi(Roszavolgyi, Budapest), by Alfredo Casella (Ricordi), by Hans von Bülow and Sigmund Lebert, translated by Theodor Baker (s/c), by Karl Krebs (s/c), by C A Martienssen (Peters), by Artur Schnabel (Curci, Milan, and Ullstein, Berlin), by B A Wallner (Henle), by Heinrich Schenker, new edition revised by Erwin Ratz (UE).

The many complete editions of the piano sonatas tend to fall into three main, though not mutually exclusive, categories: those designed primarily for use by students, those made by great pianists conveying their own principles of interpretation, and those based on the most exacting scholarly principles and aiming to give the text exactly as Beethoven left it.

In the first category the Associated Board edition by Donald Tovey and Harold Craxton holds the field by virtue of Tovey's very considerable scholarship and the penetrating musicianship and practical experience underlying his notes on each sonata. These notes are guides to execution, not analyses; his analyses are to be found in his *Companion to Beethoven's pianoforte sonatas* (see p 65). Stewart Macpherson's edition contains analyses of each work; the sonatas are also published singly. The great pianist's approach is found in the editions by Liszt, von Bülow, Bartók and Dohnányi, Lamond, and above all in that by Schnabel. This last combines the interpretative and the purely scholarly approach; it is based on authentic sources but amplifies or interprets where they are doubtful or defective and adds pedalling and fingering to achieve fidelity to the composer's intentions (Schnabel is scrupulous in distinguishing between Beethoven's dynamic marks and directions and his own). The most recent of the scholarly editions is that by B A Wallner, based on Beethoven's autographs and the original authentic editions and reproducing Beethoven's own layout even to the distribution of the notes on the stave. In this the editor follows Heinrich Schenker, who held that, where a musician of genius is concerned, the actual manner of writing provides a key to the music. Schenker was a great musical thinker as well as scholar, and his edition is preferred by some musicians to all others. Schenker also edited the last five sonatas, a separate volume to each work, with a detailed analysis (German only, UE).

The autographs of six sonatas have been published in complete facsimile: op 26, by Erich Prieger (F Cohen, Bonn); op 53, by Joseph Schmidt-Görg (Beethovenhaus, Bonn); op 57 (H Piazza, Paris); op 78 (Drei Masken Verlag, Munich); op 109 (Robert Owen Lehman Foundation, NY); op 111 (Drei Masken Verlag).

The three sonatas which Beethoven wrote at the age of twelve and dedicated to the Elector Maximilian Friedrich, KH47, in E flat, F minor and D, are published as *The three Bonn sonatas for piano*, by Felix Guenther, and separately, by John F Russell (both Francis, Day & Hunter); the two sonatinas in F and G, KH appendix 5, of which the authenticity is questionable, by F Corder (Murdoch) and with a second piano part by Henry Coleman (Augener).

Variations: Complete series by Joseph Schmidt-Görg and others (Henle), in two volumes, a popular edition of the corresponding volumes in the new CE, with a few textual notes but without the critical report, which is published separately; by Erwin Ratz (volume 1) and Monika Holl (volume 2), including a critical report (UE); volume 1 contains the more important sets. Other editions are by Adolf Ruthardt (Peters), and by Hans von Bülow and Sigmund Lebert (s/c).

Smaller groups and single works: Drei Variationenwerke, a reprint from the new GA of three of the lesser sets, by Joseph Schmidt-Görg (Henle); *The unknown Beethoven: Folk song variations for piano,* by K Herrmann (Hug, Leipzig and Zurich), three books containing all the variations of op 105 and op 107; *Drei Variationen über em irisches Volkslied* (in fact ' The last rose of summer ') op 105 no 4, *Sechs Variationen über ein österreichisches Volkslied,* op 105 no 3 and *Sechs Variationen über ein russisches Volkslied,* op 107 no 7, all by Max Bendit, with ad lib violin or flute (Schott). *Fifteen variations and fugue,* op 35 (on the ' Prometheus ' theme from his ballet music from which sprang the finale of the ' Eroica ' symphony): by Béla Bartók (Rosznyai, Budapest), by Adam Carse (Augener). *Thirty two variations in C minor,* KH80, by Hans von Bülow (s/c).

There is also the early set of *Variations on a Swiss air,* KH64, actually Beethoven's only piece for harp but published in 1790 as being for harp or piano: for harp by Nicanor Zabaleta (Schott), for piano in *Drei Variationenwerke* by Joseph Schmidt-Görg (see above). Two sets of variations for other combinations, the set on 'Se vuol ballare ' for piano and violin, KH40, and ten from the set in E flat on an original theme, for piano, violin and cello, op 44, are published as *Zwei Variationenwerke für Klavier,* by Joseph Müller-Blattau (Ichthys Verlag, Stuttgart).

Smaller pieces: All the sonatinas, bagatelles and smaller pieces other than variations are contained in a volume entitled *Klavier-*

stücke, by Otto von Irmer (Henle). The three sets of bagatelles, op 33, 119 and 126, by Paul Bekker (Drei Masken Verlag, Munich), by Carl Deis (s/c); op 33, 119 both by Béla Bartók (Rosznyai, Budapest); op 119, no editor (Peters). Among the many editions of the bagatelle ' Für Elise ', KH59 (the name is probably a mis-reading of ' Therese ', as the autograph of the little piece belonged to Therese Malfatti) are those by Carl Deis (s/c) and E Markham Lee (Murdoch, Chappell). The Rondos op 51 no 1 in C, no 2 in G, by Stewart Macpherson (Williams), the Fantasia op 77 and the 'Andante favori' in F, KH57, originally written for the ' Wald-stein ' sonata but replaced by the present slow movement, by T F Dunhill (Augener). The ' Rondo a capriccio ' op 129, ' Rage over a lost penny ', long thought to be a late work but recently shown by the discovery of the autograph to belong to the 1790's : by Erich Hertzmann, whose researches on the autograph established the date of the work (s/c), and by Alfred Brendel, with Beethoven's own title 'Alla ingharese (*sic*) quasi un Capriccio ' (UE).

Jack Werner has produced editions of a number of small pieces, some of which are of doubtful authenticity; among his indisputably genuine publications are the ' Bagatelle ' in B flat KH60 (Bosworth), the Allegretto in B minor KH61 (Curwen), the early Rondo in C KH48 (Elkin) and the Fugue in C, not listed in KH, which he has edited from the autograph in the British Museum. Another early Rondo, in A, KH49, by Alfred Mirovitch (Morris, NY and London).

Dances: Zwölf Deutsche Tänze KH13, by Edwin Fischer and Georg Schünemann (Eichmann, Berlin); a set of Dances for piano containing the six Deutsche Tänze for piano and violin KH42, the Allemande KH81 and the Waltz KH85, by Kurt Herrman (Hug, Zurich); the six Ecossaises, KH83, by Busoni (British and Con-tinental Music Agencies), by T F Dunhill (Augener), by Béla Bartók (Bárd, Budapest and Leipzig); arranged for piano duet, with the twelve Deutsche Tänze KH8, as *Ecossaisen und Deutsche Tänze für Klavier zwei Händen,* by Walter Niemann (Peters).

Pieces for organ and for mechanical clock: Orgelwerke, by Lud-wig Altman (Hinrichsen), containing the two early preludes modula-ting through all the major keys, op 39, the even earlier two part organ fugue KH31, and no 1-3 of the five pieces KH33 which

Beethoven wrote for a musical clock in Count Joseph Deym's museum; the two preludes op 39 by Adam Carse (Augener); the five pieces for mechanical clock as *Stücke für die Spieluhr,* for piano by Georg Schünemann (Schott); no 1 of these (Adagio) for wind nonet by Willy Hess (Br), for two recorders and piano by Fritz Spiegl (OUP), for cello and piano by Julius Baechi (Hug, Zurich); no 3 (Allegro) for recorder trio by Fritz Spiegl (OUP); no 5 (Minuet) for recorder quartet by Francis Grubb (Schott).

Selected recordings
of Beethoven's music

COMPILED BY BRIAN REDFERN

This list is a personal choice, but I have not included any recording which has not found favour with at least one other critic. There are many more recordings of Beethoven's music, which will give a great deal of pleasure, and the reader should not feel himself limited to those listed if he has favourite artists who are not mentioned here. However, particularly to the newcomer, I can guarantee the recordings I have selected. Under each work the recordings are listed in order of preference, although in many cases the difference between choices is very slight. At the time of final compilation (December 1969) they were all available. Inevitably by the time of publication some will have been deleted or appeared on different labels. During 1970 Deutsche Grammophon intend to issue recordings of everything Beethoven wrote and no doubt other companies will have similar ideas.

In order to avoid consultation of secondary lists and indexes I have tried to make the abbreviations of orchestral and other names intelligible on their own. Complete sets are only listed together where they are not available separately, otherwise the individual recordings in a complete set are listed separately under each work.

For each recording listed the appropriate information is cited in the order: soloist, chorus, orchestra, conductor, other music on the disc and catalogue number. Where there is a second catalogue number this is American. If there is no second number the recording is not available in America except by import. For British issues I have indicated the cheaper labels as follows; * 20/- to 30/-; † under 20/-.

Vocal music

MASSES

C major, op 86:

Vyvyan, Sinclair, Lewis, Nowakowski; Beecham Choral Soc; Royal Phil; Beecham.   ASD 280;   SG 7168.

D major, op 123 (Missa solemnis):

Janowitz, Ludwig, Wunderlich, Berry; Wiener Singverein; Berlin Phil; Karajan.   SLPM 139208-9;   DGG 139208-9.

Söderström, Höffgen, Kmentt, Talvela; New Phil Chorus & Orch; Klemperer.   SAN 165-6;   Angel S 3679 (2 recs).

Marshall, Merriman, Conley, Hines; Shaw Chorale; NBC Sym; Toscanini.   *VCM 9 (4 recs *with* Fidelio);   LM 6013 (2 recs).

Stader, Radev, Dermota, Greindl; St Hedwig's Cathedral Choir. Berlin; Berlin Phil; Böhm.   †89679-80.

OPERA

Fidelio:

Ludwig, Hallstein, Vickers, Unger, Frick, Berry, Crass; Phil Chorus & Orch; Klemperer.   SAX 2451-3, excerpts SAX 2547; Angel S 3625 (3 recs), excerpts Angel S 36168.

Nilsson, Sciutti, McCracken, Grobe, Krause, Prey, Boehme; Vienna State Opera Chorus; Vienna Phil; Maazel.   SET 272-3, excerpts SXL 6276;   London 1259 (2 recs), excerpts London 26009.

Bampton, Steber, Peerce, Laderoute, Janssen, Moscana, Belavsky; NBC Sym; Toscanini.   *VCM 9 (4 recs *with* Mass in D);   LM 6025 (2 recs).

Modl, Jurinač, Windgassen, Schock, Edelmann, Poell, Frick; Vienna State Opera Chorus; Vienna Phil; Furtwängler.   *HQM 1109-10;   Seraphim 60022 (3 recs).

SOLO VOICE WITH ORCHESTRA

Ah! Perfido—Concert aria op 65 :

Callas; Paris Conservatoire Orch; Rescigno. *Recital* *ST 690; Angel S 36200.

Jones; Vienna Op Orch; Quadri. *Recital.* SXL 6249; London 25981.

Complete:

Fischer-Dieskau; Demus.   SLPM 139216-8.

An die ferne Geliebte:

Souzay; Baldwin. (*Recital*).   SAL 3422.

Orchestral music

SYMPHONIES

1 C major:

Berlin Phil; Karajan. *With* sym 2. SLPM 138801;   DGG 138801.

Hallé Orch; Barbirolli. *With* sym 8.   *GSGC 14081;   Vanguard S 146.

Little Orch of London: Jones. *With* sym 8.   *UNS 200.

2 D major:

Berlin Phil; Karajan. *With* sym 1. SLPM 138801;   DGG 138801.

London Sym; Monteux. *With* Fidelio & King Stephen overtures. *VICS 1170.

3 E flat major (Eroica):

Berlin Phil; Karajan.   SLPM 138802;   DGG 138802.

Phil Orch; Klemperer.   SAX 2364;   Angel S 35853.

Leipzig Gewandhaus Orch; Konwitschny. †SFL 14045; SRW 19502 (6 recs all 9 sym).

4 B flat major:

Berlin Phil; Karajan.   SLPM 138803;   DGG 138803.

Vienna Phil; Schmidt-Isserstedt. *With* Consecration of the House overture. SXL 6274;   London 6512.

London Sym; Monteux. *With* Wagner's Siegfried idyll.   *VICS 1102.

5 C minor:

Berlin Phil; Karajan.   SLPM 138804;   DGG 138804.

Berlin Phil; Maazel. *With* Consecration of the House overture. †89502.

6 F major (Pastoral):

Berlin Phil; Cluytens.   ASD 433.

Phil Orch; Klemperer.   SAX 2260;   Angel S 35711.

Leipzig Gewandhaus Orch; Konwitschny. *With* sym 9.   †SFL 14035-6;   SRW 19502 (6 recs all 9 sym).

Amsterdam Concertgebouw Orch; Sawallisch. *SFM 23012.

7 *A major*:
Royal Phil; Davis. *SXLP 20038.
Berlin Phil; Karajan. SLPM 138806; DGG 138806.

8 *F major*:
Berlin Phil; Karajan. *With* finale of sym 9. SLPM 138808; DGG 138808.
Hallé Orch; Barbirolli. *With* sym 1. *GSGC 14081; Vanguard S 146.
Little Orch of London; Jones. *With* sym 1. *UNS 200.

9 *D minor (Choral)*:
Janowitz, Rössl-Majdan, Kmentt, Berry; Wiener Singverein; Berlin Phil; Karajan. *With* sym 8. SLPM 138807-8; DGG 138807-8.
Sutherland, Horne, King, Talvela; Vienna State Opera Chorus; Vienna Phil; Schmidt-Isserstedt. SXL 6233; London 1159.
Wenglor, Zollenkopf, Rotzch, Adam; Leipzig Radio Choir & Gewandhaus Orch; Konwitschny. *With* sym 6. †SFL 14035-6; SRW 19502 (6 recs all 9 sym).
Sutherland, Procter, Dermota, Van Mill; Brasseur & Eglise Nationale choirs; Suisse Rom; Ansermet. *SDD 108.

CONCERTOS—PIANO
1 *C major*:
Kempff; Berlin Phil; Leitner. SLPM 138774; DGG 138774.
Katchen; London Sym; Gamba. *With* fantasia C minor op 80. SXL 6189; London 6451.

2 *B flat major*:
Kempff; Berlin Phil; Leitner. *With* concerto 4. SLPM 138775; DGG 138775.
Arrau; Amsterdam Concertgebouw Orch; Haitink. *With* sonata op 2 no 1. SAL 3714; PHS-5-970 (5 recs—all 5 piano concertos).

3 *C minor*:
Fischer; Bavarian State Orch; Fricsay. *With* Mozart concert rondos. †89513; Heliodor S 25001.
Gelber; New Phil; Leitner. *With* sonata op 81a (Les adieux). *SXLP 20107.

94

Arrau; Amsterdam Concertgebouw Orch; Haitink. SAL 3735; PHS-5-970 (5 recs all 5 piano concertos).

4 G major:

Kempff; Berlin Phil; Leitner. *With* concerto 2. SLPM 138775; DGG 138775.

Richter-Haaser; Phil Orch; Kertesz. *With* rondo op 51 no 2. SAX 2403.

5 E flat major (Emperor):

Kempff; Berlin Phil; Leitner. SLPM 138777; DGG 138777.

Gelber; New Phil; Leitner. *SXLP 20104.

Fantasia C minor op 80:

Katchen; London Sym Chorus & Orch; Gamba. *With* concerto 1. SXL 6189; London 6451.

CONCERTOS—VIOLIN & TRIPLE

Violin D major:

Campoli; Royal Phil; Pritchard. *SXLP 20043.

Grumiaux; New Phil; Galliera. SAL 3616; Philips 900222.

Triple C major (violin, piano, cello):

Schneiderhan, Anda, Fournier; Berlin Radio Sym; Fricsay. SLPEM 136236; DGG 136236.

D Oistrakh, Oborin, Knushevitzky; Phil Orch; Sargent. *SXLP 30080; Angel S 35697.

OVERTURES

Consecration of the house, Coriolan, Egmont, King Stephen, Prometheus:

Phil Orch; Klemperer. SAX 2570.

Fidelio, Leonora nos 1-3:

Phil Orch: Klemperer. SAX 2542; Angel S 36209.

Israel Phil; Maazel. SXL 6025; London 6328.

Chamber music

WIND

March in C major (Zapfenstreich), 2 Military marches for the caroussel, Octet E flat major op 103, Rondino E flat major for wind octet, Sextet E flat major op 71:

London Baroque Ensemble; Haas. *GSGC 14038.

95

Octet E flat major op 103, Rondino B flat major for wind octet, Sextet E flat major op 71, Quintet for three horns, oboe and bassoon, March B flat major for wind sextet:
  London Wind Soloists. SXL 6170;   London 6442.
3 Duos for clarinet & bassoon op 147:
  Lancelot; Hongne. *With* septet. †TV 34076 S; Turnabout 34076.

STRING AND MIXED
Septet E flat major op 20:
  Vienna Octet. *SDD 200;   London 6132.
  Melos Ensemble. SOL 60015; Oiseau-Lyre 60015.
  Bamberg Sym Orch Chamber Ensemble. *With* clarinet & bassoon duos. †TV 34076 S; Turnabout 34076.
Sextet for 2 horns and strings E flat major op 81b:
  Berlin Phil octet. *With* Spohr. Octet. SAL 3709.
Quintet for piano and wind E flat major op 16:
  Ashkenazy; London Wind Soloists. *With* Mozart. Quintet. SXL 6252; London 6494.
2 String quintets, no 1 op 4 E flat major and no 2 C major op 29:
  Endres Quartet; Meineke (viola). *STGBY 607; SVBX 579 (3 recs *with* quintets & sextets).

STRING QUARTETS
1-6 op 18:
  Amadeus Q. SLPM 138531-3; SKL 1311-3.
1 op 18 no 1 F major:
  Smetana Q. *With* quartet 11. *SUAST 50478; Parliament S 614.
  Hungarian Q. *With* quartet 2. *HQS 1155. Seraphim S 6005 (3 recs op 18).
2 op 18 no 2 G major:
  Hungarian Q. *With* quartet 1. *HQS 1155; Seraphim S 6005 (3 recs op 18).
3 op 18 no 3 D major:
  Hungarian Q. *With* quartet 4. *HQS 1156; Seraphim S 6005 (3 recs op 18).
  Fine Arts Q. With quartet 4. †STXID 5288; Concert-Disc 210.
4 op 18 no 4 C minor:
  Hungarian Q. *With* quartet 3. *HQS 1156; Seraphim S 6005 (3 recs op 18).

Fine Arts Q. *With* quartet 3.   *STXID 5288;   Concert-Disc 210.
5 op 18 no 5 A major :
Hungarian Q. *With* quartet 6.   *HQS 1157;   Seraphim S 6005
(3 recs op 18)
6 op 18 no 6 B flat major :
Hungarian Q. *With* quartet 5.   *HQS 1157;   Seraphim S 6005
(3 recs op 18).
Janacek Q. *With* quartet 16.   *SUAST 50415;   Parliament S 623.
7-11 op 59, 74, 95 :
Amadeus Q.   SLPM 138534-6;   SKL 1314-6.
7 op 59 no 1 F major (Rasumovsky) :
Hungarian Q.   *HQS 1159;   Seraphim S 6006 (3 recs op 59,
74, 95).
Tatrai Q.   *GMA 27.
8 op 59 no 2 E minor (Rasumovsky) :
Janacek Q.   *SUAST 50616;   Parliament S 627.
Tatrai Q.   *GMA 31.
Hungarian Q. *With* quartet 11.   *HQS 1160;   Seraphim S 6006
(3 recs op 59, 74, 95).
9 op 59 no 3 C major (Rasumovsky) :
Hungarian Q. *With* quartet 10.   *HQS 1161;   Seraphim S 6006
(3 recs op 59, 74, 95).
10 op 74 E flat major (Harp) :
Weller Q. *With* quartet 11.   SXL 6148;   London 6431.
Tatrai Q.   *GMA 47.
Hungarian Q. *With* quartet 9.   *HQS 1161;   Seraphim S 6006
(3 recs op 59, 74, 95).
11 op 95 F minor :
Weller Q. *With* quartet 10.   SXL 6148;   London 6431.
Hungarian Q. *With* quartet 8.   *HQS 1160;   Seraphim S 6006
(3 recs op 59, 74, 95).
Smetana Q. *With* quartet 1.   *SUAST 50478;   Parliament S 614.
12-16 op 127, 130-132, 135 and Grosse Fuge :
Amadeus Q.   SLPM 138537-40;   SKL 1317-20.
12 op 127 E flat major :
Italian Q. *With* quartet 16.   SAL 3703;   Philips 3703.

97

4

13 op 130 B flat major:

Hungarian Q. *With* Grosse Fuge. *HQS 1178; Seraphim S 6007 (4 recs late quartets).

14 op 131 C sharp minor:

Vlach Q. *SUAST 50044; Parliament S 625.

15 op 132 A minor:

Italian Q. SAL 3638; Philips 900182.

Smetana Q. *SUAST 50885.

16 op 135 F major:

Italian Q. *With* quartet 12. SAL 3703; Philips 3703.

Janacek Q. *With* quartet 6. *SUAST 50415; Parliament S 623.

Grosse Fuge op 133:

Hungarian Q. *With* quartet 13. *HQS 1178; Seraphim S 6007 (4 recs late quartets).

TRIOS

Clarinet trio op 11 B flat major:

D Glazer (clar); Soyer (cello); F Glazer (piano). *With* Brahms, clarinet trio. †TV 34108 S; Turnabout 34108.

Trio for 3 flutes in G major, Allegro and minuet for 2 flutes G major; 6 Themes and variations for flute and piano op 105:

Rampal, Larde, Marion (flutes); Veyron-Lacroix (piano). †TV 34059 S; Turnabout 34059.

String trios op 3 E flat major, op 9 no 1 G major, no 2 D major, no 3 C minor, Serenades op 8 & op 25 both D major:

Larrieu (flute); Grumiaux Trio. AXS 3007 (3 recs); Philips 900226 (op 9 nos 1 & 3 only), 900227 (serenades).

PIANO TRIOS

1 op 1 no 1 E flat major and *2 op 1 no 2 G major*:

Beaux Arts T.—SAL 3527; Philips WS-4-007 (4 recs complete set).

3 op 1 no 3 C minor, 10 B flat major, Variations op 44 E flat major, Variations op 121a:

Beaux Arts T. SAL 3528; Philips WS-4-007 (4 recs complete set).

4 op 70 no 1 D major (Ghost), 5 op 70 no 2 E flat major, 9 E flat major:

Beaux Arts T. SAL 3529; Philips WS-4-007 (4 recs complete set).

6 op 97 B flat major (Archduke):

Beaux Arts T. *With* clarinet trio op 11 arr for piano trio. SAL 3530; Philips WS-4-007 (4 recs complete set).

VIOLIN SONATAS

1 op 12 no 1 D major:

D Oistrakh; Oborin. *With* sonata 8. SAL 3416; Philips PHS-4-990 (4 recs complete set).

2 op 12 no 2 A major:

D Oistrakh; Oborin. *With* sonata 10. SAL 3417; Philips PHS-4-990 (4 recs complete set).

3 op 12 no 3 E flat major:

D Oistrakh; Oborin. *With* sonata 7. SAL 3418; Philips PHS-4-990 (4 recs complete set).

Schneiderhan; Seemann. *With* sonatas 4 & 6. SLPM 138122.

4 op 23 A minor:

D Oistrakh; Oborin. *With* sonata 9. SAL 3419; Philips PHS-4-990 (4 recs complete set).

Schneiderhan; Seemann. *With* sonatas 3 & 6. SLPM 138122.

5 op 24 F major (Spring):

Yehudi & Hephzibah Menuhin. *With* sonata 9. ASD 389.

D Oistrakh; Oborin. *With* sonata 6. SAL 3420; Philips PHS-4-990 (4 recs complete set).

Villa; Pryor. *With* sonata 9. †MFP 2071.

6 op 30 no 1 A major:

D Oistrakh; Oborin. *With* sonata 5. SAL 3420; Philips PHS-4-990 (4 recs complete set).

Schneiderhan; Seemann. *With* sonatas 3 & 4. SLPM 138122.

7 op 30 no 2 C minor:

D Oistrakh; Oborin. *With* sonata 3. SAL 3418; Philips PHS-4-990 (4 recs complete set).

8 op 30 no 3 G major:

Szeryng; Rubinstein. *With* Brahms. Sonata 1. SB 6513; LSC 2620.

4°

D Oistrakh; Oborin. *With* sonata 1. SAL 3416; Philips PHS-4-990 (4 recs complete set).

9 op 47 A major (Kreutzer):
Yehudi & Hephzibah Menuhin. *With* sonata 5. ASD 389.

D Oistrakh; Oborin. *With* sonata 4. SAL 3419; Philips PHS-4-990 (4 recs complete set).

Villa; Pryor. *With* sonata 5. †MFP 2071.

10 op 96 G major:
D Oistrakh; Oborin. *With* sonata 2. SAL 3417; Philips PHS-4-990 (4 recs complete set).

CELLO SONATAS

1-5 op 5, 69, 102:
Rostropovich; Richter. SAL 3453-4; Philips PHS-2-920 (2 recs).

1 op 5 no 1 F major:
Janigro; Demus. *With* sonatas 4 & 5. *VSL 11062.

2 op 5 no 2 G minor:
Janigro; Demus. *With* sonata 3. *VSL 11061.

3 op 29 A major:
Du Pré; Bishop. *With* sonata 5. *HQS 1029; Angel S 36384.

Janigro; Demus. *With* sonata 2. *VSL 11061.

4 op 102 no 1 C major:
Janigro; Demus. *With* sonatas 1 & 5. *VSL 11062.

5 op 102 no 2 D major:
Du Pré; Bishop. *With* sonata 3. *HQS 1029; Angel S 36384.

Janigro; Demus. *With* sonatas 1 & 4. *VSL 11062.

HORN SONATA

Op 17 F major:
D Brain; Matthews. *Recital*. *HQM 1033; Seraphim 60040.

PIANO SONATAS

1 op 2 no 1 F minor:
Kempff. *With* sonatas 12, 19, 20. SLPM 138935; DGG 138935.

Barenboim. *With* sonatas 17, 20. *HQS 1107; Angel S 36491.

2 op 2 no 2 A major:
Kempff. *With* sonata 3. SLPM 138936; DGG 138936.

Backhaus. *With* sonatas 10, 19.   SXL 6359;   London 6585.
3 op 2 no 3 C major:
   Kempff. *With* sonata 2.   SLPM 138936;   DGG 138936.
   Rubinstein. *With* sonata 23.   SB 6633;   LSC 2812.
   Barenboim. *With* sonata 15.   *HQS 1185.
4 op 7 E flat major:
   Backhaus. *With* sonatas 25, 31.   SXL 6300;   London 6535.
   Kempff. *With* sonatas 9, 10.   SLPM 138938;   DGG 138938.
5 op 10 no 1 C minor:
   Kempff. *With* sonatas 6, 7.   SLPM 138937;   DGG 138937.
   Arrau. *With* sonatas 6, 7.   SAL 3550.
   Ferber. *With* Balakirev. Sonata, & Liszt. *Chants polonais.* †STXD
5273.
   Barenboim. *With* sonatas 6, 7.   *HQS 1152.
6 op 10 no 2 F major:
   Kempff. *With* sonatas 5, 7.   SLPM 138937;   DGG 138937.
   Arrau. *With* sonatas 5, 7.   SAL 3550.
   Barenboim. *With* sonatas 5, 6.   *HQS 1152.
7 op 10 no 3 D major:
   Kempff. *With* sonatas 5, 6.   SLPM 138937;   DGG 138937.
   Arrau. *With* sonatas 5, 6.   SAL 3550.
   Barenboim. *With* sonatas 5, 6.   *HQS 1152.
8 op 13 C minor (Pathétique):
   Kempff. *With* sonatas 14, 23.   SLPM 139300;   DGG 138941
(*with* sonatas 14, 15, 24).
   Serkin. *With* sonatas 14, 23.   SBRG 72148;   MS 6481.
   Rubinstein. *With* sonatas 14, 26.   SB 6537; LSC 2654.
   Badura-Skoda. *With* sonatas 14, 23.   *XLP 20055;   Westminster
14274.
   Firkusny. *With* sonata 14.   †MFP 2068;   Pickwick S 4024 (*with*
sonatas 14, 23).
9 op 14 no 1 E major:
   Kempff. *With* sonatas 4, 10.   SLPM 138938;   DGG 138938.
   Arrau. *With* sonatas 10, 19, 20, 25.   SAL 3611.
10 op 14 no 2 G major:
   Backhaus. *With* sonatas 2, 19.   SXL 6359;   London 6585.
   Kempff. *With* sonatas 4, 9.   SLPM 138938;   DGG 138938.

Arrau. *With* sonatas 9, 19, 20, 25.   SAL 3611.

11 op 22 B flat major :

Richter. *With* sonatas 19, 20.   *SFM 23014;   Philips 900076.

Kempff. *With* sonatas 13, 27.   SLPM 138939;   DGG 138939.

12 op 26 A flat major :

Kempff. *With* sonatas 1, 19, 20.   SLPM 138935;   DGG 138935.

Richter. *With* sonata 23.   *VICS 1427;   VICS 1427.

Backhaus. *With* sonata 18.   SXL 6064;   London 6366.

13 op 27 no 1 E flat major :

Kempff. *With* sonatas 11, 27.   SLPM 138939;   DGG 138939.

Schnabel. *With* sonatas 14, 15.   COLH 56.

14 op 27 no 2 C sharp minor (*Moonlight*) :

Kempff. *With* sonatas 8, 23.   SLPM 139300;   DGG 138941 (*with* sonatas 8, 15, 24).

Rubinstein. *With* sonatas 8, 26.   SB 6537;   LSC 2654.

Schnabel. *With* sonatas 13, 15.   COLH 56.

Serkin. *With* sonatas 8, 23.   SBRG 72148;   MS 6481.

Badura-Skoda. *With* sonatas 8, 23.   *XLP 20055;   Westminster 14274.

Firkusny. *With* sonata 8.   †MFP 2068;   Pickwick S 4042 (*with* sonatas 8, 23).

15 op 28 D major (*Pastoral*) :

Kempff. *With* sonatas 21, 24, 25.   SLPM 139301;   DGG 138941. (*with* sonatas 8, 14, 24).

Barenboim. *With* sonata 3.   *HQS 1185.

Schnabel. *With* sonatas 13, 14.   COLH 56.

16 op 31 no 1 G major :

Kempff. *With* sonatas 18, 22.   SLPM 138940;   DGG 138940.

17 op 31 no 2 D minor :

Richter. *With* Schumann. Fantasia.   ASD 450;   Angel S 35679.

Kempff. *With* sonatas 26, 28.   SLPM 138942;   DGG 138942.

Barenboim. *With* sonatas 1, 20.   *HQS 1107;   Angel S 36491.

18 op 31 no 3 E flat major :

Backhaus. *With* sonata 12.   SXL 6064;   London 6366.

Kempff. *With* sonatas 16, 22.   SLPM 138940;   DGG 138940.

19 op 49 no 1 G minor :

Barenboim. *With* sonatas 26, 32.   *HQS 1088.

Kempff. *With* sonatas 1, 12, 20.   SLPM 138935;   DGG 138935.

Richter. *With* sonatas 11, 20.   *SFM 23014;   Philips 900076.

Backhaus. *With* sonatas 2, 10.   SXL 6359;   London 6585.

Arrau. *With* sonatas 9, 10, 20, 25.   SAL 3611.

20 op 49 no 2 G major :

Kempff. *With* sonatas 1, 12, 19. SLPM 138935;   DGG 138935.

Richter. *With* sonatas 11, 19.   *SFM 23014;   Philips 900076.

Arrau. *With* sonatas 9, 10, 19, 25.   SAL 3611.

Barenboim. *With* sonatas 1, 17.   *HQS 1107;   Angel S 36491.

21 op 53 C major (*Waldstein*) :

Kempff. *With* sonatas 15, 24, 25.   SLPM 139301;   DGG 138943 (*with* sonatas 23, 25).

Backhaus. *With* sonata 23.   SXL 2241;   London 6161.

Barenboim. *With* sonata 31.   *HQS 1181;   Angel S 36581.

22 op 54 F major :

Kempff. *With* sonatas 16, 18.   SLPM 138940;   DGG 138940.

23 op 57 F minor (*Appassionata*) :

Richter. *With* sonata 12.   *VICS 1427;   VICS 1427.

Kempff. *With* sonatas 8, 14.   SLPM 139300;   DGG 138943 (*with* sonatas 21, 25).

Rubinstein. *With* sonata 3.   SB 6633;   LSC 2812.

Backhaus. *With* sonata 21.   SXL 2241;   London 6161.

Serkin. *With* sonatas 8, 14.   SBRG 72148;   MS 6481.

Badura-Skoda. *With* sonatas 8, 14.   *XLP 20055;   Westminster 14274.

24 op 78 F sharp major :

Kempff. *With* sonatas 15, 21, 25.   SLPM 139301;   DGG 138941 (*with* sonatas 8, 14, 15).

25 op 79 G major :

Backhaus. *With* sonatas 4, 31.   SXL 6300;   London 6535.

Kempff. *With* sonatas 15, 21, 24.   SLPM 139301;   DGG 138943 (*with* sonatas 21, 23).

Arrau. *With* sonatas 9, 10, 19, 20.   SAL 3611.

Foldes. *With* piano concerto 5.   †89598.

26 op 81a E flat major (*Les adieux*) :

Barenboim. *With* sonatas 19, 32. *HQS 1088;   Angel S 36424 (*with* sonatas 8, 14).

Kempff. *With* sonatas 17, 28.   SLPM 138942;   DGG 138942.

Rubinstein. *With* sonatas 8, 14.   SB 6537;   LSC 2654.

27 op 90 E minor:

Kempff. *With* sonatas 11, 13.   SLPM 138939;   DGG 138939.

Solomon. *With* piano concerto 4.   XLP 30020;   Seraphim S 60016 (*with* piano concerto 1).

28 op 101 A major:

Bishop. *With* sonata 30 & small pieces.   *HQS 1017;   Seraphim S 60035.

Kempff. *With* sonatas 17, 26.   SLPM 138942;   DGG 138942.

29 op 106 B flat major (Hammerklavier):

Kempff. *With* sonata 30.   SLPM 138944;   DGG 138944.

Ashkenazy.   SXL 6335;   London 6563.

30 op 109 E major:

Bishop. *With* sonata 28 & small pieces.   *HQS 1017;   Seraphim S 60035.

Hess. *With* sonata 31.   *XLP 30005.

Kempff. *With* sonata 29.   SLPM 138944;   DGG 138944.

31 op 110 A flat major:

Hess. *With* sonata 30.   *XLP 30005.

Kempff. *With* sonata 32.   SLPM 138945;   DGG 138945.

Backhaus. *With* sonatas 4, 25.   SXL 6300;   London 6535.

Barenboim. *With* sonata 21.   *HQS 1181;   Angel S 36581.

32 op 111 C minor:

Kempff. *With* sonata 31.   SLPM 138945;   DGG 138945.

Barenboim. *With* sonatas 19, 26.   *HQS 1088.

MISCELLANEOUS PIANO PIECES

Diabelli variations op 120:

Bishop.   SAL 3676;   Philips 900220.

Brendel.   †TV 34139 S;   Turnabout 34139.

Bagatelles op 33, op 119, op 126:

Brendel.   †TV 34077 S;   Turnabout 34077.

Bagatelles op 126, Ecossaises E flat major, Rondo a capriccio op 129 G major, 2 Rondos op 51, Für Elise, Andante favori F major Variations G major on ' Nel cor piu ':

Kempff.   SLPM 138934;   DGG 138934.

Andante favori F major, Bagatelles op 126, Für Elise, Ecossaises E flat major, 32 Variations C minor:

    Foldes. †89514.

Variations on: ' *God save the king* ', ' *Rule Britannia* ', *theme from* ' *Ruins of Athens* ', *Für Elise, Rondo a capriccio op 129 G major Ecossaises E flat major, Andante favori F major, Polonaise C major, Klavierstück B flat major*:

    Brendel. †TV 34162 S.

... ...

Index

109